Engineering Happiness

Engineering Happiness

*A New Approach for Building
a Joyful Life*

Manel Baucells and Rakesh Sarin

UNIVERSITY OF CALIFORNIA PRESS

Berkeley Los Angeles London

University of California Press, one of the most distinguished university presses in the United States, enriches lives around the world by advancing scholarship in the humanities, social sciences, and natural sciences. Its activities are supported by the UC Press Foundation and by philanthropic contributions from individuals and institutions. For more information, visit www.ucpress.edu.

University of California Press
Berkeley and Los Angeles, California

University of California Press, Ltd.
London, England

Library of Congress Cataloging-in-Publication Data

Baucells, Manel, 1966–
Engineering happiness : a new approach for building a joyful life / Manel Baucells and Rakesh Sarin.
    p.   cm.
Includes bibliographical references and index.
ISBN 978-0-520-26820-3 (cloth : alk. paper)
ISBN 978-0-520-26821-0 (pbk. : alk. paper)
1. Happiness.   I. Sarin, Rakesh, 1948–   II. Title.
BF575.H27B38 2012
152.4'2—dc23

2011034436

Manufactured in the United States of America

20   19   18   17   16   15   14   13   12   11
10   9   8   7   6   5   4   3   2   1

The paper used in this publication meets the minimum requirements of ANSI/NISO Z39.48-1992 (R 2002) (*Permanence of Paper*).

To my parents—Manel
To Anna, Kavita, Ravi, Kyle, and Katelyn—Rakesh

Our stable sources of happiness

CONTENTS

An annex to this volume, "The Mathematics of Happiness," is available online at www.ucpress.edu.

PREFACE

Engineers on Happiness

We are what our deep, driving desire is. As our deep, driving desire is, so is our will. As our will is, so is our deed. As our deed is, so is our destiny.
             —Upanishad

Socrates and Aristotle regarded the human desire to be happy as self-evident. All subordinate goals—including health, wealth, and virtue—are sought because they ultimately lead to happiness. In turn, data shows that happy people tend to be healthier, live longer, and have better social relationships. The pursuit of happiness explains the billions of dollars spent each year on consumer goods, from cosmetics and fashion apparel to computers and new cars. Who among us does not want to be happy?

In recent years, lots of books on happiness have been written. This one is different.

This is a book on happiness written by engineers. Engineers love to solve puzzles. Engineers at play have solved countless puzzles and given the world amazing things such as skyscrapers, bridges, cars, televisions, planes, computers, and cell phones. Engineers have built useful and beautiful things to alleviate pain and suffering and to increase the comfort, well-being, and even happiness of all. That got the two of us thinking about the nature of happiness, and we ventured the question: Can happiness itself be engineered?

Simply put, engineers strive to understand, quantify, and manipulate the physical world from computer chips to steel. Engineers play with physical objects, discover their underlying properties, and create formulas to predict their behavior. Would the same mind-set work for something as elusive as happiness?

Perhaps you're thinking: "What can two pointy-headed math geeks possibly teach me about happiness?" As any good, curious engineers would do, the two of us set out to define, measure, and discover the properties of happiness in a systematic and analytical way. Our curiosity has led us to some fascinating findings, the most important of which is our belief that happiness can, in fact, be engineered.

We begin with the crucial observation that

HAPPINESS *equals* REALITY *minus* EXPECTATIONS

We call this the fundamental equation of happiness. In order to engineer happiness, we propose a set of six laws that govern our emotions. We call them the laws of happiness. Each of these laws modifies the fundamental equation of happiness, making it more precise and applicable to a wide range of life choices. Our claim is that through planning and acting on these six principles, happiness becomes a controllable and predictable possibility.

To some, happiness is like a pendulum. It may swing back and forth, but will always return to the center. According to this view, there is not much one can do to fundamentally change our base level of happiness. Our view is different. We argue in this book that happiness is like a sailboat. Indeed the wind and ocean currents influence its movements, but you have the control of the rudder. Without your exerting control, the sailboat drifts. Our laws of happiness serve as the rudder that will help you guide your sailboat to a happier destination.

The very essence of attaining a joyful life is a *choice*. Once you understand the nature of happiness and master its laws, as described in this book, we believe that you can lay the groundwork for building an amazing life brimming with happiness.

ACKNOWLEDGMENTS

Leticia Camilher Camargo has been our research assistant for this project. Her main task was to dig up the large literature on happiness and connect all the scattered ideas with our framework. Along the way, Leticia has provided many lively stories and examples and has helped make the book more readable. Her contribution has been essential.

Craig Boreth did an excellent job of editing and rearranging the material to improve the flow of ideas. Madeleine Adams provided the final quality control through her careful copy editing.

IESE Business School and UCLA's Anderson School of Management provided financial assistance for this project.

Ralph Keeney, from Duke University, saw the need for including concrete guidelines on how to be happy. Following this recommendation, we wrote the chapter "Building a Happier Life." Ana García Bertrán, our translator into Spanish, gave us suggestions for improving the flow of the original version. Melissa L. Caldwell, from UC Santa Cruz, made suggestions on incorporating cultural influences on happiness.

Vivien Steger and Theodore Treantafelles helped in editing and rewriting some of the stories in the book. Anna Yang and Kavita Sarin provided valuable input.

Many other colleagues and friends have helped us along the way: Kelly See, from NYU, for pointing us toward research on stability of relationships; Ada Ferrer-i-Carbonell, from the Universitat Autònoma de Barcelona, for her important research and hospitality. Other colleagues who read the book and gave suggestions are Silvia Bellezza, a PhD candidate from Harvard, Steven Lippman from UCLA, Robin Keller from UC Irvine, Mike Norton from Harvard Business School, and Peter Wakker from Erasmus University.

Eva Maria Lozano provided the nice tocometer recording. Xavi Viladiu converted the book into audio format, which helped the revision. Lucia Ceja helped us improve our understanding of flow and engagement; Connor O'Neill brought to our attention karma yoga; and Gigi Le suggested the word *crescendo* to us. Sonia Clotet and German Loewe read the manuscript and made many insightful comments.

Several of the stories in the book are real. Here are their direct or indirect contributors: Juan Carlos Castañeda, Maite Mijancos, Eduardo Martinez-Abascal, Irene Perdomo, Marta Raurell-Ramoneda, and Xavi Viladiu.

Many friends have enthusiastically read the book and given us suggestions. Among them are Francesc Baucells, Albert Farré, Grace Lau, Susy Masià, Roger Romance, Daniel Smith, and Marta Ventura.

INTRODUCTION

The Science of Happiness

Shall we be merry?   —Shakespeare

Who among us has not dreamed of winning the lottery or coming into
great wealth, thus ensuring a life of carefree bliss and never-ending
happiness for the rest of our days? After all, if we just had that bottom-
less bank account, all of our worries and insecurities would fade into the
distance like the runway beneath our new Gulfstream G650 private jet.
Does happiness really work that way? Can it be bought, despite what the
old cliché says? Here's the story of one man who lived the dream, and
his answer is a resounding "No."

Andrew Jackson Whittaker Jr. grew up very poor in Jumping Branch,
West Virginia. He started working full-time at the age of fourteen. He
never had a car or a TV until much later in life, but through hard work
he started a successful plumbing company. "We have managed to bring
water to almost 100,000 people," he said, referring proudly to his successful career. Jack's was an American success story, and he considered
himself a happy man. In 2002, good fortune *really* touched Jack's life, or
so one would think. On Christmas Day, Jack became America's richest
lottery winner ever, winning the $315 million Powerball jackpot.

Jack promised that his newly won fortune would be shared with the
church and the poor. His beloved granddaughter Brandi said she just
wished to have a new car and meet the hip-hop singer Nelly. The scenes

broadcast on national television that Christmas season seemed to be the beginning of a fairytale life.

Jack and his wife, Jewell, opted for the lump-sum payment of more than $170 million rather than annual payments. So after taxes, they received close to $112 million. Indeed, they donated 10 percent of the money to several churches in West Virginia. Jack also bought a house for the woman who had sold him the ticket and rehired twenty-five employees he had had to lay off the previous month.

Two years later, Jack was back in the news, but this time for a sad update on his life. He had been arrested twice on drunk-driving charges, was ordered into rehab, and was involved with gambling and prostitution schemes. Five years later, his wife had left him and his granddaughter, Brandi, had died as the result of drug addiction after falling into bad company and letting go of old friendships.[1]

How did Jack's happy life—which he'd worked so hard to build from nothing—end up spiraling out of control? Even though he was a wealthy man before the jackpot, it seems that the huge windfall was overwhelming. The unplanned spending and the inability to deal with his unexpected fortune turned him into a rich poor man.[2] Now, years down the road, he says that he regrets winning the lottery. Surely, whatever went wrong with Jack cannot possibly happen to us. Or can it?

Happiness, it turns out, is far too complex to be bought with mere lottery winnings. It takes a much deeper understanding of our own minds and motivations to find greater happiness in our lives. Think of happiness as a jigsaw puzzle. We are all given many pieces and we must ourselves discover how they all fit together for us.

So, how much can science help us in solving the puzzle of happiness? The science of measuring, calculating, and predicting happiness is still in its infancy. A growing body of research demonstrates that the brain on its own is not prepared to figure out how to be happy and can easily be led down false paths. Marketers in our society recognize this and cleverly create the illusion that buying their products will make us happy. The responsibility of knowing what really makes us happy is ours, not theirs.

Our goal with this book is to help you understand what drives your own happiness. We've developed a set of six major principles, which we call the laws of happiness, to explain how happiness works and why it is so often elusive. Understanding these laws will help you recognize the happiness triggers in your life, avoid the happiness traps all of us face every day, and lay the groundwork for a consistently happier life.

Just as the laws of motion govern the physical world, the laws of happiness govern the mental world. These laws of happiness, though much less precise than the laws of physics, are universal and apply uniformly to all human beings.

Happiness, in our conception, includes all shadings of feelings, emotions, and states of mind. The very word *happiness* conjures up different meanings for different people. In the social sciences and the humanities, there is a lively debate about whether the terms *happiness, satisfaction, well-being,* and *pleasure* connote the same thing. We use them interchangeably, however. In our framework, happiness is the theoretical sum of pleasures and pains or positive and negative emotions and states of mind over an extended period of time. The origin of this definition of happiness can be attributed to Jeremy Bentham (1748–1832), who is regarded as one of the fathers of modern economics. More recently, the Nobel laureate Daniel Kahneman has argued that experienced utility that sums the momentary pleasures and pains over time is a more appropriate measure of happiness than the retrospective evaluation of happiness that is often used in surveys. In the next chapter we will discuss in some detail the progress that has been made in measuring happiness.

We acknowledge that cultures and individuals do not share a common set of values that contribute to their happiness. Furthermore, the pursuit of happiness may not be the chief goal of every individual. When Prince Siddhartha set out on his epic journey, he was not seeking happiness. Instead, he sought and attained enlightenment. Mother Teresa defined her mission in life as caring for "the hungry, the naked, and the homeless." Henry David Thoreau and John Muir favored the simple freedom of living in nature over material entrapments. In different cultures, people value lifestyles and goals that may not be shared by Western culture. Although we believe the laws of happiness are universal, the goals and criteria for happiness may differ across historical, political, and economic contexts.

In spite of many factors that make each of us different, there are large similarities among individuals. The laws of happiness are drawn from this set of similarities. To prove that these similarities hold across cultures and times, this book complements the findings from scientific experiments with examples from ancient literature and pearls of wisdom from the world's religions that support our laws of happiness.

Think of the two of us, the authors of this book. We were born and raised in different countries, India and Spain. We were reared in different religions, Hinduism and Catholicism. These large differences in culture and background make us perceive many things differently. We both, however, believe in the existence of a universal set of principles governing emotions. The laws of happiness apply equally to both of us.

Remember, happiness is not a capricious outcome of destiny or fortune, like winning the lottery, but is the result of how our mind operates in making decisions. Through planning and acting on the laws of happiness, happiness becomes a controllable possibility rather than an unattainable goal in a consumer-oriented society.

The key premise of this book is that the very essence of attaining a happier life is *choice*. You can choose to live wisely by following the six laws of happiness and engineering a happier life for yourself, but it requires skill and determination.

Our ancestors believed that happiness was controlled by luck, fate, or the gods and was beyond human control. The historian Darrin McMahon writes, "it was only in the eighteenth century that human beings took upon themselves exclusive responsibility for happiness, casting aside both God and fortune, severing the ties that had long held happiness to forces over which we have no control."[3]

Bentham, who may be regarded as a father of both economics and psychology, was perhaps the first Western scholar who provided a calculus of happiness. To Bentham, happiness was the positive balance of pleasure over pain. He wrote, "Nature has placed mankind under the governance of two sovereign masters, *pain* and *pleasure*. It is for them alone to point out what we ought to do, as well as to determine what we shall do." He further proposed a way to calculate total happiness by assigning values to the intensity, duration, and other attributes of pleasure and pain, and then summing up the totals of each to compute the net balance of utility.[4] Though Bentham's mathematical precision was impeccable, measurement of subjective states such as pleasure and pain was seriously lacking in his time.

Since Bentham, several writers have expressed their views on the important role of happiness in our lives. John Stuart Mill refined Bentham's ideas, arguing that some pleasures are of higher quality than others; this view has been disputed by Bertrand Russell and others, who consider it elitist.[5] The prominent psychologists William James and Abraham Maslow both had views on happiness, but neither had an interest in the calculus of happiness.[6]

The inflection point in happiness research came in the 1970s, when both economists and psychologists turned their attention to measuring happiness. In the early 1970s, the economist Richard Easterlin collected a large amount of data and questioned whether economic growth improves human well-being.[7] About the same time, the psychologists Philip Brickman, Dan Coates, and Ronnie Bullman measured the happiness of lottery winners and paraplegics. They concluded that lottery winners were not particularly happy and that paraplegics were much less unhappy than most people would anticipate.[8] David Lykken, based on the largest comparative study of twins to date, concluded that well-being and happiness are "at least 50 percent inherited."[9]

Armed with millions of observations from almost all the countries of the world, researchers have begun to decipher the causes and correlates of happiness. There is unanimity of findings that for a person to be happy some basic needs, such as for food, shelter, safety, and social relationships, must be satisfied. There are some stable findings, as well, that marriage has a strong positive effect on happiness and that unemployment is a major cause of unhappiness. Psychologists have measured feelings as they fluctuate over time and during different activities. People seem to like sex most and commuting least. In spite of a large amount of data, however, a skeptic might still question the reliability of measuring pleasure and pain or positive and negative emotional experiences and states of mind.

Pleasure and pain are the "go" and "stop" of our biological, emotional programming. The view that pleasure and pain are private events—and therefore cannot be measured—is widely held but incorrect. The measurement of subjective experiences, such as the loudness of a sound or how hot or cold something is, are topics in the well-established field of psychophysical research. Psychophysical functions that govern the pleasure of drinking sugar water and the pain from an electric shock are orderly and comparable across different people.

Reports of well-being can be supplemented by physiological indicators of emotional quality and intensity, ranging from objective measurements of subtle facial expressions to measuring the activity in the prefrontal cortex of the brain. At some point in the near future, there might even be handheld devices that use biochemical and neurological measurements to indicate the quality of well-being at a given moment.

Our approach to studying happiness is rooted in the literature of decision analysis and management science. This literature seeks to solve well-formulated decision problems—problems for which the link between the possible actions and their consequences is perfectly understood. The two of us have been conducting research on happiness for the past ten years, with the goal of setting happiness as a well-formulated decision problem. Components of our work have been published in scientific journals in our field. This book provides for the first time a comprehensive and accessible discussion of our framework and its key results for the curious reader.

. . .

In a Native American legend,[10] an old Cherokee is teaching his grand-son about life. "A fight is going on inside me," he says to the boy. "It is a terrible fight between two wolves. One is evil—he is anger, envy, greed, guilt, and false pride. The other is good—he is joy, peace, love, hope, and kindness."

The grandson thinks about this for a minute and then asks, "Which wolf will win?" The old Cherokee replies, simply, "The one you feed."

PART I

Overview

CHAPTER I

Measuring Happiness

> When you can measure what you are speaking of and express
> it in numbers, you know that on which you are discoursing.
> But when you cannot measure it and express it in numbers,
> your knowledge is of a very meagre and unsatisfactory kind.
> —Lord Kelvin, English physicist and mathematician

As with matter and energy, our understanding of happiness increases with the discovery of more and more precise measurement instruments. The great milestones of science, such as deciphering the motion of heavenly bodies, all began with the measurement of the object being studied. Without measurement, it is not possible to advance our understanding of the complex dynamics of the happiness seismogram.

There are at least seven ways to measure happiness. Each one helps to create a picture of what makes people happy. Let's see how these seven measurement devices work and the main findings each provides.

RECALL-BASED SELF-REPORTS

The primary strategy for measuring happiness is very simple but has proven to be very useful. It is as easy as asking people twice a year the simple question: All things considered, how satisfied are you with your life as a whole these days? Would you say that you are very happy, pretty happy, or not too happy?

It may seem too simplistic an approach, and it is. It gives only an imprecise estimate of the *average* height of the happiness seismogram. The usual finding is that people are generally happy. We surveyed 103 people from Spain. In one of our questions, we asked them to rate their happiness on a 1 (low) to 10 (high) scale, and found that two-thirds gave an answer of 7 or higher.

Many researchers have developed more sophisticated self-report studies, attempting to take a more valid measurement of happiness. Ed Diener of the University of Illinois has conducted many such studies.[1] He uses the following multiple-item questionnaire:

Indicate on a 1–7 scale [1 = strongly disagree, 7 = strongly agree] your agreement with each statement:

   a. In most ways my life is close to my ideal.
   b. The conditions of my life are excellent.
   c. I am satisfied with my life.
   d. So far I have gotten the important thing I want in life.
   e. If I could live my life over, I would change almost nothing.

The average of the five scores is a measure of happiness. Such a measure is more precise than the measurement based on one question. Diener and colleagues have taken pains to show that these self-reported measures of well-being correlate reasonably well with other measurements of well-being, such as bodily measurements (levels of stress), evaluation of our happiness by friends and relatives, smiling, and experience sampling.[2] Of course, self-reports can be biased in many ways. For instance, the emotion of the moment can have a disproportionate influence on the answer. If your partner is away on a long business trip, the momentary loneliness might lead you to answer that you are not that happy, even though you actually are. But, even taking the imprecision and potential for bias into account, the existing research suggests that, for many purposes, self-reported well-being is a useful indicator of individual happiness.

The usefulness of self-reports comes mostly from the vast quantity of data that have been collected using this method. Because collecting self-reports is cheap and easy, there is an ever-growing record of measurements taken in different countries, at different times, and from subjects experiencing all sorts of circumstances. These results comprise the content of the World Database of Happiness and the World Values Survey.[3]

Studies based on these databases suggest that, across different countries, happiness is high among people with lots of friends, the young and the old, married and cohabiting people, the healthy, and the self-employed. Income has a moderate effect, although, as we will soon see, it is *relative* income that matters the most. Through this kind of approach, scientists have found that American millionaires living in huge, luxurious houses are barely happier than Masai warriors in Kenya who live in huts.[4] Other research has attempted to put a price tag on overcoming adversity, suggesting that it takes millions of dollars to make up for the emotional turmoil of a relationship breakup or a job loss.

Another interesting finding is the relationship between happiness and age. When are we the happiest in our lives? The economists David Blanchflower and Andrew Oswald tried to answer this question, examining data on well over a half million people from about seventy-two countries, both developed and undeveloped.[5] They found that happiness follows a U-shaped curve over our lifetimes, or, for the more optimistic among us, a smile-shaped curve. In either case, happiness appears to dip to its lowest level in middle age.

They suggest that, on average, the low point of happiness occurs around age forty-four. The exact age varies from nation to nation and between genders, but it is always somewhere in middle age. After reaching middle age, happiness begins increasing, and by the time you reach an average of fifty years old, you can expect to be on the bright side of the curve again.

Although this U-shaped trend in happiness is certainly fascinating, it doesn't tell us anything about the causes of our happiness or why it should dip steadily until midlife before rising again.

One possibility is that individuals learn to adapt to their strengths and weaknesses, and are happier in the second half of their lives after accepting their limitations and giving up on early aspirations that cannot be met. It could also be that cheerful people systematically live longer than unhappy people, although that wouldn't account for the decline in happiness leading to middle age.

What about the effect of education? If we compare a person who has not completed high school with a college graduate, the more educated person will be on average 0.3 standard deviations higher in the happiness bell curve. If happiness were measured as in the SAT test score, with the average at 600 points, then the less educated would have a 585 and the more educated a 615. In our knowledge-based society, education has a moderate but positive effect on happiness.[6]

Happiness and Productivity

The December 2007 edition of *Perspectives on Psychological Science* features the work of researchers from the University of Virginia, the University of Illinois, and Michigan State University. Scholars analyzed the behaviors and attitudes of 193 undergraduate students at the University of Illinois and observed data from the World Values Survey.[7]

Among the conclusions drawn was that those who classify themselves as 8 or 9 on a 10-point scale were more successful in some aspects of their lives than those who consider themselves to be 10 on the happiness scale. People who are just "too happy" may be less inclined to alter their behavior or to adjust to external changes even when such flexibility offers an advantage.

"The highest levels of income, education, and political participation were reported not by the most satisfied individuals (10 on the 10-point scale)," the authors wrote, "but by moderately satisfied individuals (8 or 9 on the 10-point scale)."

The 10s earned significantly less money than the 8s and 9s. Their educational achievements and political engagement were also significantly lower than those who considered themselves to be moderately happy or "happy-but-not-blissful." In other words, being joyful all the time does not necessarily provide any drive to succeed.

Happy people tend to be optimistic, and even though this is a good characteristic, it could mislead people to view their symptoms too lightly, seek treatment too slowly, or simply not look into what could be a happier future just because the present is good enough now. The bottom line is that if you are perfectly fine with the way things are going, then you most likely won't want to do anything to change.

Income and Happiness

These large surveys on life satisfaction allow us to look at the relationship between money and happiness. Here are the two questions for which we have answers: Are richer countries happier than poorer countries? Are rich people happier than poor people?

The answer to the first question is as follows. If a poor nation moves from $4,000 to $5,000 in income per capita, its life satisfaction increases significantly. No surprises here. However, if a nation five times richer moves from $20,000 to $21,000 in income per capita, the effect of the same $1,000 increase on happiness is tiny. To experience the same increase in happiness, the rich nation needs an increase of $5,000 in income per capita. In poor countries, additional income is mostly spent on basic goods. Hence, money does matter a lot for happiness. In rich countries, additional income is mostly spent on adaptive goods, whose effect on happiness is temporary. (On the distinction between basic and adaptive goods, see the end of chapter 4.)

If we look at the evolution of happiness as the income per capita increases, we see a similar pattern (see figure 1). Once the income per

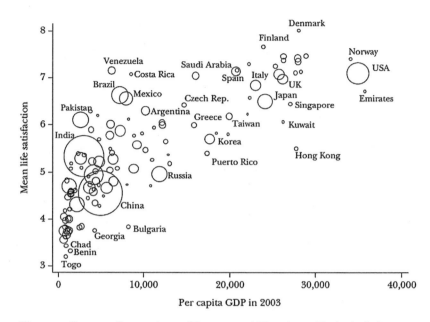

Figure 1. Country Comparison of Income and Happiness. Each circle is a country, with diameter proportional to population. GDP per capita measured in purchasing power parity–chained dollars at 2000 prices. Source: Pen World Tables 6.2

capita reaches a minimum threshold of around $20,000, the effect of additional income on happiness becomes very small. Thus, there is a large increase in happiness up to the income level that is required to satisfy the basic needs and only a moderate increase beyond that level.[8]

Let's move to the second question. Are rich people happier than poor people? We can compare the happiness of the rich and the poor in a given country at a given moment. This analysis shows that the rich are significantly happier than the poor. This holds true for both rich and poor countries. Social comparison explains these data quite well. Thus, as a country becomes richer its total happiness increases until the income per capita exceeds $20,000. Past this point, the total happiness of the country increases very little with increases in income. Nonetheless, regardless of the average income, within the country, the richer are happier than the poor because of the effect of social comparison. This implies that for a moderately affluent individual, an increase in money does increase happiness, but it does so mainly because of social comparison.

For lack of better measures, income and gross domestic product have been used as rods to measure the success of a society. The former president of Harvard Derek Bok argues that research on happiness can inform public policy and potentially aid in improving citizens' quality of life.[9] He examines the policy implications of happiness research for economic growth, equality, retirement, unemployment, health care, mental illness, family programs, and education. In the United Kingdom, Richard Layard advocates that the goal of public policy is to maximize happiness.[10] Income is important to the extent that it contributes to happiness. For instance, devoting public funds to improve mental health may be more happiness-efficient than using these same resources to improve infrastructure. Layard also claims that, when it comes to happiness, policies that produce stability may be more important than those that produce growth.

On March 18, 1968, Robert F. Kennedy challenged conventional wisdom in saying that the gross national product (GNP) measures everything except that which makes life worthwhile.[11] Forty years later, the tiny kingdom of Bhutan (nestled between India and China) adopted gross national happiness (GNH) in place of GNP as the measure for tracking its progress. Economic indicators such as GNP focus largely on market transactions and thus are biased in favor of production and consumption. In contrast, GNH attempts to measure the quality of human experience and well-being in its totality. Along with living standards, GNH includes education, health, good governance, ecology, culture, time use, community vitality, and psychological well-being in order to measure the progress of a country. His Majesty King Khesar, the fifth Druk Gyalpo of Bhutan, ended his coronation address with a prayer "that the sun of peace and happiness may forever shine on our people."[12]

Culture and Happiness

Surveys over several years have consistently revealed that Danes are happier than Americans. Though one can speculate about the reasons why Denmark and other Scandinavian countries score near the top in level of satisfaction, one must be cautious about cross-cultural comparisons. Researchers have examined, for example, whether the word *satisfied* in English and *tilfreds* in Danish could convey different meanings.

An intriguing finding from the survey data is that, in spite of an endowment of more favorable objective factors that are usually associated with well-being, such as vacation days, health care availability, and income per capita, French people show a lower level of life satisfaction than Danes. We do not resolve the question of whether Danes are truly happier than French, which someday may be settled through neurobiological methods; instead, we focus on how an individual living in Denmark or in France could improve his or her level of happiness through choices that are informed by our laws of happiness.[13]

DAY RECONSTRUCTION METHOD

Surveys are the easiest and most widely used method to measure total happiness, but we would like to have a closer view of how happiness changes during the day. In other words, we would like to observe how the happiness seismogram goes up and down over time.

The Nobel Prize–winning psychologist Daniel Kahneman pioneered a new kind of happiness measurement approach, based on measuring, analyzing, and comparing how people spend their time and what kinds of affective experiences they have during distinct activities.[14] Participants keep a diary of everything they do during the day, from reading the paper when they wake up to commuting, and even arguing with their bosses. Then they list their activities from the previous day, noting whom they were with, and rate the episodes on a range of feelings on a seven-point scale. The method aims to learn about people's daily lives and to rate how satisfied or annoyed, sad or joyful they felt.

A study using the day reconstruction method given to more than nine hundred women in Texas produced some surprising results.[15] The women ranked the five most positive activities as being (in descending order) sex, socializing, relaxing, praying or meditating, and eating. Exercising and watching TV were not far behind (ahead of shopping and talking on the phone), but at the other end, curiously, taking care of their children ranked below cooking and only slightly above housework. Commuting was the lowest ranked activity.

This order may seem surprising, considering that parents tend to say their children are their biggest source of joy. Does that mean that parents are systematically lying about how much they enjoy raising their children? It is more likely the case that the joy of raising children is derived more from looking back and considering a lifetime of achievements rather than performing the day-to-day tasks of parenting. In other words, the daily grind of taking care of children—cleaning up after them, making sure they brush their teeth, and so on—is not necessarily a primary source of happiness, but the overall experience of being a parent may ultimately create a great deal of happiness.

Your happiness depends on not only what you are doing but also with whom. The same study that ranked the happiness derived from certain activities found that, on average, people enjoy their friends' company the most and, not surprisingly, their boss's the least. As we have all experienced, good company enhances the quality of any good experience. You enjoy the view from the beach, the concert, or even the cup of coffee more if you share those experiences with the right people.

The day reconstruction method takes all of these activities and social factors into account—as well as other factors, such as how well rested you are, which greatly influences day-to-day happiness—and determines an average rating of happiness throughout a given day. Looking at the evolution of happiness during the day, we conclude that the subjects of this study are not morning people, they really enjoy their lunch hours, and their happiest time is at the end of the day. Sound familiar?

Keep in mind that this study surveyed only women, so we have to be careful about generalizing based on the results, but it is a useful reminder of how much our happiness can change from moment to moment within a day.

As we have seen, recall-based self-reports and the day reconstruction method can produce very insightful results. But these methods can be unreliable, introducing bias into the results. Let's take a look at a method of measuring happiness that does not rely on memory.

EXPERIENCE SAMPLING METHOD

Grace is an architect. She is deep in concentration, designing the staircase for a conference center. Suddenly, she is distracted by a beeper on her belt, which reminds her that she is supposed to complete a short questionnaire describing what she is doing at this moment and her current emotional state.

In the 1980s, hundreds of volunteers just like Grace agreed to carry beepers and "be bothered" at random times during the day. When the beeper sounded, these volunteers might have been commuting, in a meeting, writing on the computer, answering e-mails, or taking care of their children.

This "experience sampling" method is more complex to arrange and administer than the day reconstruction method, but it has the advantage of measuring the happiness experience in the moment (what we will call *moment-happiness*) directly, rather than relying on potentially faulty memory.

Using the experience sampling method, the psychology professor Mihály Csíkszentmihályi (pronounced "chick-sent-me-high-ee") made a major discovery in the area of happiness. By measuring the moment-happiness of his subjects directly, he noticed that their minds, when left unoccupied, wandered in chaotic ways from one state to another, often drifting toward negative feelings of boredom, anxiety, and depression. Analyzing the data, he identified the conditions that produced and sustained a particular positive state of mind, in which subjects reported being most happy. He called this state *flow*. According to Csíkszent-mihályi, the mind naturally enters into a state of flow when (1) one is engaged in a task that is directed toward a goal, (2) the task poses a challenge (neither too easy nor too difficult), and (3) one receives feedback on progress toward the goal. During this state of mental engagement, time stops and all negative emotions are blocked. Given that the state of flow is both predictable and sustainable, Csíkszentmihályi essentially discovered a predictable method to eliminate negative feelings and increase happiness.[16]

One study using the experience sampling method found the flow phenomenon to be remarkably common, regardless of culture, race, gender, or age. Elderly Korean women, Japanese teenage motorcycle gang members, Navajo shepherds, assembly-line workers, artists, athletes, and surgeons—all describe the experience in essentially the same words. To experience flow we must find the challenge in what we are doing and then focus on doing it as well as we can.

Obviously, creating flow is easier said than done, but understanding how it works allows us to increase the likelihood that the necessary conditions for flow (and happiness) will at least be present in our daily lives.

Using smart phones, Matthew A. Killingsworth and Daniel T. Gilbert of Harvard University collected a large sample of experiences and associated happiness. They also measured "mind wandering."[17] Their database currently contains nearly a quarter million samples from about five thousand people from eighty-three different countries who range in age from eighteen to eighty-eight and who collectively represent every one of eighty-six major occupational categories. Their findings confirm what had been found previously: happiness is high during sex, exercise, or socializing, or while the mind is focused on the here and now, and low during commuting or while the mind is wandering.

SUICIDE RATES

Believe it or not, suicide rates can be a reliable measure of happiness. According to a study by Mary Daly and Daniel Wilson of the Federal Reserve Bank of San Francisco, suicide rates correlate with many of the findings on the self-report measurement of happiness.[18] Essentially, those experiences that make people happy lead to a decline in suicides, whereas experiences that make people unhappy cause an increase. For example, an increase of 1 percent in the unemployment rate increases the male suicide rate from 20 per 100,000 to about 46 per 100,000. Interestingly, there is a huge difference between male and female suicide rates—men are five times more likely to take their own lives—suggesting that, overall, women are happier than men.

Of course, to say that suicide is caused by unhappiness is in one sense obviously true but in another sense is an oversimplification. Certainly, happy people would not take their own lives, but people who are so unhappy that they would consider suicide are probably dealing with some form of mental illness. The English novelist Virginia Woolf, who committed suicide in 1941, left a suicide note expressing just how happy her life had once been, and her awareness that her mental illness stole that happiness. She wrote to her husband, Leonard, "I don't think two people could have been happier till this terrible disease came." Obviously, suicide rates represent a very blunt instrument with which to measure happiness, but they can provide some insight into the nature of happiness. Not surprisingly, suicide rates decrease with education and increase with the availability of firearms. When it comes to money buying happiness (or in this case, lack of money creating unhappiness), the authors found that *relative* income is more important than simply how much money someone makes. If the wealthiest 10 percent of the population gets richer, the suicide rate increases, confirming the impact of envy. On the other hand, if the poorest 10 percent of the population gets richer, suicide rates decrease. Indeed, the study is titled "Keeping Up with the Joneses and Staying Ahead of the Smiths: Evidence from Suicide Data."

STUDIES OF DIARIES

Another method of measuring happiness, albeit one that requires a certain degree of luck, is to analyze personal diaries. The epidemiologist David Snowdon is famous for the so-called Nun Study, a longitudinal study primarily of aging and Alzheimer's disease. He studied the diaries of 678 Roman Catholic nuns.[19]

Although the diaries were first studied as part of Snowdon's research on Alzheimer's, the findings also turned out to be a rich source of information for psychologists trying to understand the effects of positive thinking and aging. They searched the writings for words that connote positive emotions (such as *happiness, love, hope, gratitude,* and *contentment*) and negative ones (*sadness, hatred, fear, confusion,* and *shame*). The results were impressive: This analysis showed that only one in seven of the melancholic nuns made it to their eighty-fifth birthdays, but nine out of ten of the happy nuns made it to that age. They concluded that the happy nuns lived an average of nine years longer than the unhappy ones (by comparison, nonsmokers live only three years longer than smokers).

Many other fascinating studies lend credence to these findings and support a link between happiness and physical well-being. Happy people tend to have higher levels of cortisone and other immunological defenses. Critically ill patients who are more optimistic tend to have (on average) better outcomes. One study even found that people who rated themselves as happy were able to keep their hands soaked in a bucket of ice-cold water for a much longer time than those who rated themselves as unhappy.

BODY MEASUREMENTS

Can you guess which physical activity uses forty-two different muscles moving at the same time? The high jump? The backstroke? Performing Bach's Prelude and Fugue in A minor? The answer is: smiling. The seemingly simple act of smiling is actually a complex, coordinated physical maneuver. And, more amazing, it is practically universal among human beings. In the 1960s, the psychology researcher Paul Ekman sought to explore the universal nature of emotions.[20] While visiting isolated communities in Papua New Guinea, he confirmed that these indigenous people express emotions just as we do in Western cultures: shedding tears in sad moments or smiling when happy. Ekman found that there are nineteen distinctive ways of smiling, but only one of them is genuine, the so-called Duchenne smile.[21] Even though it looks very similar to fake smiles, it is in fact slightly different because the muscles that generate it and the orders coming from the brain to make them move are distinct. Only when the ocular muscles at the corners of your eyes move does it mean that you are truly smiling out of happiness. All the other expressions are forced smiles of politeness, fear, sympathy, or some other emotion. Real smiles are involuntary and automatic, meaning that when we feel pleasure they naturally appear. In other words, the frequency and duration of Duchenne smiles could be a possible "objective" way to measure happiness.

Ekman conducted extensive cross-cultural studies of facial expressions in places as diverse as Papua New Guinea, the United States, Japan, Brazil, Argentina, Indonesia, and the former Soviet Union. He showed photographs of facial expressions to people in different cultures and countries and asked them to judge the emotion underlying each facial expression. Across cultures there was agreement on the facial expressions associated with happiness, anger, disgust, and sadness. Even in isolated cultures such as those of the Dani of Indonesia and the Fore of New Guinea, who do not even have words for emotions, people correctly identified the emotion shown by a facial expression. The tool

Ekman developed for measuring facial movement in anatomical terms has been used by numerous scientists.

Ekman's studies have revealed that, although we all may share expressions for certain emotions, we may differ greatly on what triggers them. Ekman posits that culture influences emotions in three ways. The first is display rules: what emotions can be shown to whom and in which contexts. Coping mechanisms to deal with emotions such as anger may also vary by culture. Finally, the triggers of emotions are also culturally variable.

NEUROIMAGING

While observing genuine smiles is a decidedly low-tech method of measuring happiness via bodily measurement, these days we may also avail ourselves of remarkably high-tech methods, such as directly observing brain activity using functional magnetic resonance imaging, or fMRI.

Using this technology, researchers at University College of London found that people describing themselves as "truly, deeply, madly" in love not only rate their happiness higher but also have the brain waves to prove it.[22] Volunteers had their brains imaged while they looked at photos of their romantic partners. As the subjects stared at the pictures, their brains lit up in areas that also activate during euphoria. Apparently, these intense romantic feelings make people very happy—head over heels or, more accurately, brain over heels!

The neuroscientist Richard Davidson sought to find which parts of the brain are associated with positive and negative emotions.[23] He placed volunteers into an fMRI machine, induced positive and negative emotions with pictures and video clips, and observed their brain activity. He found that positive feelings correlate with brain activity on the left side of the prefrontal cortex, whereas negative feelings correlate with brain activity on the right side of the prefrontal cortex. The prefrontal cortex is somewhere in the front of our brains and above the ears.

In our quest to measure happiness objectively and precisely, these measures of brain activity seem to present the most promising advance to date. Future technological advances will no doubt provide more precise measurement of happiness, but for now the most satisfactory and seemingly valid measurement of moment-happiness is the difference in prefrontal cortex activity between the left and right sides of the brain, or "left–right brain asymmetry."[24] Thus, we observe:

Our moment-happiness can be approximated by the difference in the levels of electrical activity on the left and right sides of the prefrontal cortex.

After examining the brain activity of monks who had extensive meditation experience, Davidson found that the monks had actually altered the structure and function of their brains and were happier than the average person. He also found that senior monks had greater left–right brain asymmetry than their junior counterparts. This suggests that it's not just that happy people are drawn to the monastery but that meditation and the monastic life may have made them happier. Of course, other passionately pursued endeavors may have the same effect, but for these men meditation did the trick.

Of all the people he measured, Davidson found that the French Buddhist monk Matthieu Ricard rated the highest in the difference between left and right prefrontal cortex activities, thus putting himself in the running for happiest man on Earth. And all without lottery winnings, flat-screen TV, or designer clothes.

CHAPTER 2

Defining Happiness

Happiness is intended pleasure and the absence of pain;
unhappiness is pain and privation of pleasure.
—John Stuart Mill

We believe it is possible to define happiness in mathematical terms. In
the same way that energy is measured in calories, happiness can in principle be measured in what we call happydons. The building blocks we
use to define happiness are emotions, feelings, and states of mind.

Happiness is composed of the momentary feeling we all have when
things are going our way, when the weather is beautiful, or when our
favorite team just won the big game. And unhappiness is composed of
the unpleasant feeling we all have when we get a bad grade or catch flu.

Rather than thinking of happiness as a momentary emotion, which
can change from moment to moment, think of total happiness as the
net balance of your emotions over time. As we will soon argue, happiness will be defined as the total sum, over time, of momentary emotions. Positive emotions increase happiness; negative emotions decrease
happiness. So, the extent to which positive emotions outweigh negative
ones would describe your level of overall happiness. The increase and
decrease in happiness is proportional to the time and intensity with
which these emotions are experienced.

Emotions, feelings, and states of mind are the basis for the study
of happiness because they are universal, common to all people. Most

biologists would agree with Darwin's point that men and animals share many basic emotions such as fear of an enemy or pleasure of a food. Of course, while the capacity to experience and express emotions and feelings is a universal capacity of human beings, the display of these emotions may vary across cultures.

To get a better sense of how this would work, from an engineering viewpoint, it would be helpful to visualize the nature of emotions relative to one another. Luckily, the psychology professor James Russell has developed a method by which inner states or emotions can be drawn on a map.[1] In Russell's model, each emotion can be placed as a point on a map, with a horizontal axis measuring how positive or negative the emotion is and the vertical axis showing how calm or excited that emotion makes us (see figure 2).[2] We will use the horizontal axis, negative versus positive, as the basis to define happiness.

As you move from left to right on the map, the emotions go from negative (such as depression) to neutral to positive (hope). From bottom to top, emotions go from low arousal (boredom and peace of mind) to high arousal (anger and passion).

On the map of emotions, we have tried to include the most basic emotions we feel, such as anger, fear, pain, envy, hope, pride, and love.[3] If you were able to zoom in on the map, then more detail on each state would be visible. For example, if you zoomed in on *pain,* then you would be able to see many forms of pain, such as headache, fever, back pain, and indigestion. If you zoomed in on *enlightenment,* then you could observe different states such as the introspective contemplation of art, of natural wonder, or of mathematical beauty; or mental clarity such as the feelings of understanding and discovery of basic truths.

Just as heat can be felt with varying intensities, the same can be said for emotions such as joy, anxiety, pleasure, fear, and comfort. As the intensity of an emotion changes, so does its position on the map. Relief, for example, can take different positions in the map—the relief of knowing that you actually do have exact change at the market has a different intensity than the relief of finding out that a biopsy came back negative.

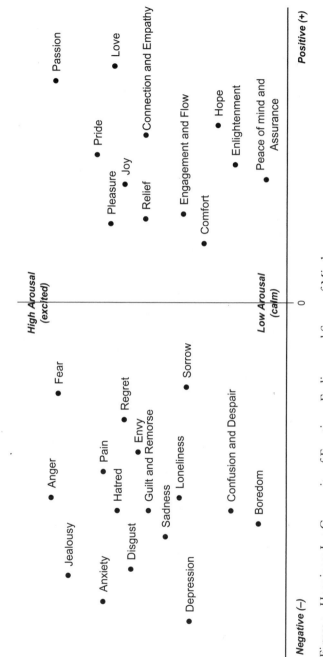

Figure 2. Happiness Is a Composite of Emotions, Feelings, and States of Mind

Using the map, we can get a quantitative sense of just how happy we are at one particular moment, reading the intensity of the emotion of the moment in the positive vs. negative dimension. We refer to this variable as *moment-happiness.*

Moment-happiness or unhappiness is given by the intensity of positive or negative emotion experienced at the moment.

But moment-happiness fluctuates all the time depending on what's going on in our lives. We may be perfectly content during a family dinner, scared after seeing a spider, or sad after reading a story in the newspaper. It is also possible to be in a neutral state. Then we have a zero value of moment-happiness. But soon, a phone call, a thought of what is to come, a memory, an experience, will take us out of this neutral state and change the moment-happiness. Total happiness must take into account this ongoing roller-coaster of emotions. In Hindu and Buddhist tradition, feelings are generally described as one of three types: pleasant *(sukha),* unpleasant *(dukkha),* and neither pleasant nor unpleasant *(asukha-adukkha).* Elimination of unpleasant feelings *(dukkha)* or suffering is the main aim of Buddhism.

AN OPERATIONAL DEFINITION OF HAPPINESS

The pleasure or pain at a particular moment cannot be taken as a measure of happiness. Moment-happiness is very volatile and prone to outside influences. To truly get a sense of overall happiness, we would need to measure the intensity and duration of moment-happiness over an extended period of time, similar to the way a seismograph measures motion in the ground.

This way of measuring happiness may seem a bit contrived, but there already exists a measuring device that illustrates the principle: the tocometer.

A tocometer is a pressure gauge strapped to a birthing mother's abdomen. It records the physical strength of labor contractions and draws them on a graph. The peaks on the graph represent the strongest contractions and thus the moments of greatest pain. The tocometer is a reliable device to record the pain experienced, as self-reports of pain felt during contractions correlate well with the height of the graph.

What is the total pain experienced during labor? A simple answer, one that takes into account the entire recording, is that the total pain experienced during the labor would be the area under the graph. Equivalently, it is equal to the average height of the graph multiplied by its duration.

The tocometer measures the moment intensity of the mother's pain during childbirth. Consider a hypothetical instrument that resembles a tocometer, except it records *all* the different emotions that we may experience. This ideal device can be called the *happiness seismograph,* a device that could record on a time line the intensity of the feeling at each moment and produce a happiness seismogram.[4] The scale will take positive values for positive emotions and negative values for negative emotions. The assumptions here are that we can experience only one emotion at a time and that the intensity of all emotions can be plotted on a common scale.

As engineers, we want to define happiness *operationally.* For our purposes, the operational definition of happiness is just the area on the seismogram between the graphed line and the zero line.[5] Actually, since the seismogram can be either positive or negative, total happiness is the area above the zero line minus the area below the line of the graph. Simply stated, total happiness is the sum total of pleasures minus pains.[6] This is equivalent to the average intensity of moment-happiness multiplied by its duration.

Total happiness is the net area between the graph of the happiness seismogram and the zero line, that is, the average level of moment-happiness multiplied by the duration of the experience.

To further quantify happiness, we need to define the different levels of intensity on the seismogram. To make it simple, our scale goes from

−10 (extremely unhappy) to +10 (extremely happy). For example, +10 happydons could be the happiness experienced by the soccer players of the Spanish team after winning the World Cup. The average intensity over a specified period of time measures total happiness, in units we are calling *happydons*. Thus, a player on the Spanish team who stayed at intensity +10 in moment-happiness for two hours experienced a total of 20 happydons during those two hours.

THE HAPPINESS SEISMOGRAM

The idea of using seismographlike technology to measure emotions has been around for a long time. In 1881, the economist Francis Edgeworth wrote:

> To precise the ideas, let there be granted to the science of pleasure what is granted to the science of energy; to imagine an ideally perfect instrument, a psychophysical machine, continually registering the height of pleasure experienced by an individual. . . . From moment to moment, the height of pleasure registered by this machine varies, the delicate index now flickering with the flutter of the passions, now steadied by intellectual activity, low sunk whole hours in the neighborhood of zero, or momentarily springing up towards infinity. The continually indicated height is registered by photographic or other frictionless apparatus upon a uniformly moving vertical plane. The quantity of happiness between two epochs is represented by the area contained between the zero-line.[7]

To see how this hypothetical happiness seismograph would work, let's take the example of a particularly exhilarating life experience: skydiving.

A group of students had just spent long hours studying for an intense week of examinations. When the term was over, they were finally able to enjoy some free time. They decided to have fun and try something a little crazy: skydiving! Over the next few days, they arranged the details of the trip. During this time, anxiety and excitement mounted as they started exchanging pictures and videos of skydivers they found on the Internet. The friends gathered for dinner the night before the jump, with everyone eagerly looked forward to the event. But the next morning, on the actual day of the jump, their enthusiasm had given way to fear; they felt their stomachs flip at the idea of jumping out of a plane. Some were even contemplating backing out of the adventure.

As soon as they parked the car at the local airport, this group of students was impressed by what they saw. The sky was dotted with skydivers coming from all directions toward the field in which they stood. Suddenly, a parachute landed extremely fast in front of them, frightening this already shaken group of friends. As they signed waivers and got instructions from the professionals, their eagerness to jump increased, as did their anxiety, which now even made their hands and foreheads sweat as they boarded the small plane. Once airborne, they heeded the instruction that they were not to look out the window toward the ground but instead to look only at the clouds, in order to avoid getting dizzy. As they sat for the next fifteen minutes in the crowded airplane filled with backpacks, gear, and a lot of nervous people, their minds seemed to be an open stage for all kinds of thoughts—from early childhood memories, to what they ate for breakfast (which was making their stomachs upset), to the thought of what would happen if the parachute didn't work properly. Then the door opened and a rush of cold wind blew into the plane, giving everybody the feeling that it was now or never—they just had to do it!

One after another, together with their instructors, the students jumped out of the plane. Within seconds, they were flying with their arms spread open in midair, screaming and enjoying the energy of a free fall. The parachutes deployed properly. Everyone wafted downward and landed safely on the green field. As they rejoined, each person was awash in a sea of emotions: excitement, shock, a sense of accomplishment, and relief that left them smiling nonstop for the next hour. On the way home and for the next few days, they revisited and recounted the sensation and the excitement of jumping, and discussed about how soon they would all jump a second time!

This overall experience is crowded with emotions of varying types and degrees. Using a happiness seismograph, we could measure and calculate the happiness of this experience (see figure 3). Imagine a sketch of how all these different emotions would be recorded by a happiness seismograph.

A positive emotion, such as the enthusiasm of the skydiving experience, with an intensity of +3 sustained for 5 hours, would add 15 happydons to one's overall happiness. And a negative emotion of average intensity −7, such as the student's fear, sustained for 2 hours, would subtract 14 happydons. Keep in mind that we're not as concerned about the absolute value of the measurement, but rather the relative value that allow us to compare experiences.

Let's look back at the skydiving example and calculate how much happiness the students obtained from their experience.

Emotion	Average Intensity	Duration (hours)	Happiness
Stress	−2.5	6	−15
Excitement	2	3	6
Assurance	3	4	12
Agitation	−2	6	−12
Enthusiasm	3	5	15
Anxiety	−2	7	−14
Fear-Panic	−7	2	−14
Relief	4	9	36
Joy	4	5	20
Pride	2	13	26
TOTAL HAPPINESS	+60		

It is clear from the skydiving example that maximizing total happiness does not imply that we must avoid pain and anxiety at all costs. Often, one needs to "invest" in activities that may temporarily cause unhappiness to "harvest" happiness in the long run. For example, going to school and taking exams may be stressful but in the long run the hard work may pay off in terms of better job opportunities. Or dieting to later

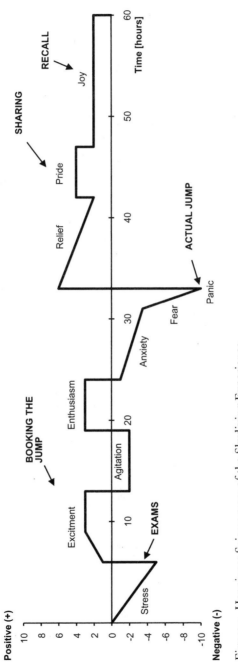

Figure 3. Happiness Seismogram of the Skydiving Experience

stay fit and avoid health complications. In each of these cases, total happiness can be calculated by the sum of the positives minus the negatives.

We must acknowledge that defining total happiness as the sum-area of moment-happiness poses some philosophical issues. For instance, it assumes that emotions of different nature can be compensated. Thus, one hour of headache at level −3 can be compensated for with one hour of pleasurable relaxation at level +3.

It must also be acknowledged that the maximization of total happiness is not the only goal in life. Indeed, a virtuous life may not be easily reduced to a seismogram of happiness. But a meaningful and virtuous life also doesn't have to be an unhappy one. As we come to understand the laws of happiness, we will be able to improve our enjoyment of life without sacrificing our ethical and virtuous conduct.

THE COMPLETE SEISMOGRAM
OF AN EXPERIENCE

Looking at the map of the seismogram, observe that the actual moment of the jump was powerfully negative. But because the duration of panic was very short, it did not significantly detract from the total happiness derived from jumping. In fact, it turns out that the experiences *before* jumping (excitement, anxiety) and *after* jumping (relief, pride, bragging rights) actually contribute more to the skydiver's overall happiness than the jump itself does.

To further explore how events may result in counterintuitive happiness seismograms; let's look at two experiences that would seem to be easily categorized as positive and negative: going on vacation and going in for surgery. We generally think of vacation as a pleasant experience and surgery as an unpleasant one. In reality, both experiences generate periods of positive and negative moment-happiness before and after the event.

After booking a holiday, we often enter a period of positive anticipation as we look forward to going away to a new place. As the departure date approaches, we realize that we still have to take care of unfinished business at work, pack the suitcase, water the plants, and take the cat to the neighbors' house. Therefore, the anxiety builds until finally we depart and begin the holiday. Our happiness declines further when the flight is full of noisy children, reaching an all-time low when we arrive at the hotel and find that the room does not have the view we hoped for, there is no swimming pool, and the hot water in the shower is lukewarm. The following day, after a good night's sleep, things begin to look up and we find that we very much enjoy the rest of the holiday. Once we return home, the holiday is just a memory. We spend a few days feeling miserable because we do not like being back at work very much and have a mountain of emails to attend to, and then we readapt to our old routine and look back on the holiday with fondness.

When you are booking a vacation you can look at it as buying an emotional roller-coaster. In contrast to a vacation, the anticipation of a surgery is likely to be filled with dread. As the time approaches we may feel less unhappy as we are more distracted with preparations. The surgery itself is probably less traumatic than we expect; still, it is bound to have unpleasant periods. As for postsurgery, our mood tends to improve as the pain wears off. We appreciate the good care received. If the outcome of the surgery is good then we enjoy improved health and alleviation of pain. We find ourselves grateful for these blessings and this adds to our happiness.

All three of the previous examples—the skydiving, the vacation, and the surgery—illustrate the power of anticipation and recall in determining how much happiness an experience can produce.

ANTICIPATION

Which day of the week are people most happy? One would expect that people are happier during the weekend than on any of the working days of the week. This is generally true, but there is one exception. In an article conveniently titled "Utility from Anticipation and Memory," the economists Jon Elster and George Loewenstein report the following experiment.[8] When asked to rank the days of the week in order of their liking, most students put Friday ahead of Sunday, even though there are classes on Friday and none on Sunday. Friday benefits from their anticipation of the weekend to come, while Sunday suffers because of the workweek ahead.

Anticipation of good experiences increases the moment-happiness before the experience, and anticipation of bad experiences decreases the moment-happiness before the experience.

According to this principle, it makes sense to delay good events and speed up bad ones. In another experiment with thirty American undergraduate students, Loewenstein found that the students preferred to delay a hypothetical kiss from their favorite movie star, presumably to harness some pleasure from the anticipation. The same students preferred to hasten a mild electric shock and get it over with quickly.[9] If you must swallow a bitter pill, then do it right away. Therefore, the optimal way for delivering news is to make sure the bad news comes first and is not given too much emphasis, and then it should be followed by emphatic good news.

People hate waiting for bad news. This should be taken into account, for example, when announcing layoffs. When a company needs to fire some of its employees, the process should be carried out as quickly as possible and the cuts should be made all at once. For the remaining employees, it is important not to give the impression that there is more bad news to come. The same applies to the release of other bad news. If possible, it is better to release the information only when it is possible to say "all this is now behind us."

The anticipation of a good event creates happiness but also increases expectations. This means that if the event is cancelled or it is not as good as anticipated, we may be disappointed. For example, when going on a date, more often than not, people end up disappointed because their minds may have created an unrealistic picture of how the date would go. People often protect themselves from too much anticipation by holding down their expectations. As the saying goes, "Don't count your chickens before they are hatched."

RECALL

William Stanley Jevons, one of the followers of Bentham, suggested that feelings of pleasure and pain are prompted by three distinct experiences, namely:

1. The anticipation of future events.
2. The sensation of present events.
3. The memory of past events.

We've just discussed how anticipation can contribute to happiness or unhappiness. Let us now consider recall and the happiness derived from the memory of past events.

The memory of the pleasure derived from a great distinctive meal, a visit to one of the Seven Wonders of the World, or a romantic interlude may last for a lifetime. The happiness seismogram for such events is dominated by anticipated and recalled pleasures, much like our skydiving example. Adventure travelers often report that the hardships endured during their trips eventually result in their fondest memories. In contrast, memories of a childhood trauma could be debilitating for many years and may even require professional help to soothe the pain.

Happiness or unhappiness from recall is only important while we can still remember the experience; once it has been forgotten we can no longer derive happiness from it. Hence, the question is: what makes certain episodes stick in our memory?

In an exciting study, scientists for the first time recorded the individual brain cells that are active in recalling a memory. They found that a spontaneous memory resides in the same neurons that had fired most furiously back when the event was experienced. As you recall seeing a

Tasmanian devil in a zoo, certain neurons in your brain become active. These are the same neurons that were ignited when you first encountered the Tasmanian devil in a cage in that zoo.[10]

When asking people what makes them happy, they often describe some moment in which they were especially happy. Those peak moments may be short, but they produce a stream of pleasant recollections. Daniel Kahneman and his collaborators have found that people rarely remember the duration of a good or bad experience, but rather they recall the emotions they felt during the *peak* and the *end* of the experience. The negative recall from your last visit to the dentist may depend, not on whether the procedure lasted ten minutes or one hour, but rather on the moment of maximum discomfort or pain.[11] Peak moments are recalled because our brain cells are most active when we experience these events.

Happiness and unhappiness from recall depends on memory. We tend to remember peak moments, or moments of intense positive or negative emotion, regardless of the duration of these experiences.

Since recalling happy moments produces happiness, and high-intensity emotions tend to stick more in our transient memory, we would be wise to pursue these moments of intense happiness from time to time; and avoid experiences of intense unhappiness. Pursuing short-lived high emotions is beneficial to our happiness because those moments provide us with durable memories. Of course, we need to strike the right balance between these occasional, highly charged experiences and our day-to-day happiness.

Reminiscing about past pleasurable experiences such as skydiving, the birth of a child, or a stroll with your lover adds to present happiness. In some cultures, such as in India, customs require sharing of good news with neighbors and the community. Then, there will be multiple opportunities to recall over time as the same event, such as a wedding, is discussed again and again in conversations with those with whom the news was overtly shared.

One specific family we know seems to understand anticipation and recall very well. This family takes vacations every two years. They spend one year searching for a destination and planning activities. After they return from their vacation, they take the following year to edit and share their vacation pictures and videos with friends and relatives. This family knows that planning and reminiscing contribute at least as much to total happiness as the trip itself. In essence, they are able to squeeze as much happiness from their vacation as possible.

Happiness from anticipation and happiness from recall are somewhat in conflict. If one increases, the other decreases. Why is that? Anticipation of an event such as a fabulous birthday party in Las Vegas, elevates the seismogram before the event and increases the expectation. Therefore, it decreases the impact of the actual experience, which is now less of a surprise. Hence, as the intensity of emotion is lower, it is less likely to be remembered and enjoyed afterward. This explains why surprise parties are so memorable. Thus, we may want occasionally to find in our lives surprising positive events that will become memorable.

This same logic applies to bad news. It is not always clear which is better: to give bad news all of a sudden, or let it trickle out little by little. A balance between anticipation, adaptation, and recall needs to be determined in deciding the approach. When we give the bad news all of a sudden, the recipient can avoid the anxiety of anticipation. Of course, the bad news can trigger such intense negative emotions that it lasts in memory for a long time. For instance, the sudden death of President Kennedy was a much more memorable event than the anticipated death of President Reagan.

Therefore, if we prepare the person for some bad news they will experience negative anticipation, in the form of anxiety or worry. But when they actually get the bad news, it is less of a surprise; they can better deal with the situation and avoid the negative recall.

Hence, there is no clear-cut recipe for how to deliver good and bad news. We can, though, create possible seismograms of these negative events and suggest which approach would produce a higher average level happiness (or, more likely in this case, a lower level of *un*happiness).

SUMMARY

Recall your first kiss—hopefully, your experience was pleasurable. Now, recall a time when you stumbled and fell, scraping your knees—that burning sensation was surely a painful experience. Most of the time, we can easily decide whether a particular experience, and its associated emotion, is on the positive or the negative side. We can also compare experiences. We can say with some confidence that getting a wisdom tooth extracted is more painful than overclipping your nail. The pain of a breakup cannot be compared to that of fracturing a bone. The nature, intensity, and duration of pain experienced during a breakup and during a fracture are quite different. Is it conceivable to use a common unit to compare this variety of experiences?

If you ask a person, "How are you feeling right now?" you can estimate the sign and the intensity of the affective experience at that moment. Most people will be able to state whether they are experiencing a positive emotion (joy, love, hope) or a negative emotion (sadness, hatred, despair) at any given moment. They may also be able to report the intensity of their emotion, although only approximately.

Happiness is a consequence of those momentary positive and negative emotions. The scale we have introduced ranges from intensely positive to neutral and from neutral to intensely negative. A positive moment-happiness when you just wake up may arise because you had a good night's sleep, or because you glanced at the face of a sleeping child. It may also occur because you recalled a funny dream or anticipate the vacation that you will be taking later that week. For our purposes, the exact nature or cause of the emotion is not important. We're concerned with its intensity and duration.

We define total happiness as the average intensity of emotions multiplied by their duration. Looking at a seismogram for a life event, total happiness is the net area under the graph (the total area produced by positive emotion minus the total area produced by negative emotion).

Having shown how to measure and define happiness, we now introduce the six laws of happiness. The six laws will help us understand the direction and intensity of our emotions, and thus allow us to control our happiness seismogram. These laws are universal, meaning that they apply to a wide range of life situations. We will provide findings from scientific experiments, examples from ancient literature, and pearls of wisdom from the world's religions to support our laws of happiness.

PART II

Laws of Happiness

CHAPTER 3

The First Law of Happiness

Relative Comparison

Annual income twenty pounds, annual expenditure nineteen
six, result happiness. Annual income twenty pounds, annual
expenditure twenty pounds and six, result misery.
—Charles Dickens

Happiness and unhappiness are colorful experiences: think of each
emotion on the map of feelings and emotions as a particular type of
flower, which, together with many other flowers, forms a diverse garden.
Because a particular feeling can have several levels of intensity, we can
think that any given type of flower having different shades of color. All
of our different emotions, each with multiple levels of intensity, will fill
in the map of emotions.

Our inner life is like a butterfly that moves from flower to flower in
this garden of inner states. Where it goes or where it chooses to stop
is difficult for us to predict. At times, it will remain for long hours at a
single position, and at others it may pay a quick visit to a random flower.
The butterfly may favor different flight patterns during the day or night,
or exhibit certain tendencies over the years. This butterfly is not alone.
The inner lives of the people around us are butterflies as well, which
also move around this garden, and the movement of each one affects the
others in complex ways.

Feelings and emotions make up the very matter that forms happiness. The intensity of the emotion at a point in time is the moment-happiness. Total happiness is the sum of the moment-happiness over a specified time period. But can we really think of emotions as tangible and predictable? One day you are happy; the next day you get the blues. An activity you used to enjoy a lot may no longer be fun, but a person you once found boring may become a trusted friend with whom you enjoy spending time. The feelings and emotions we will experience are precisely the pieces of a yet-to-be-solved puzzle.

People in Ancient Greece thought that being happy was a matter of luck or fate up to the whims of the gods; therefore, they felt they had no control over it. They used the word *eudaimonia*, which roughly means "good spirits," to describe emotions.

When our predecessors first contemplated the movement of the planets, they saw a complexity that was difficult to understand. Some of them, astronomers such as Tycho Brahe and Johannes Kepler, were not intimidated and started to record data and track the movements of the moon, the planets, and the stars. The big jump in our knowledge of motion occurred in 1687, when Isaac Newton published *Principia*.[1] In this monumental work, Newton presented the laws of motion of bodies: a short set of rules that, taken at face value, explained a wide range of accumulated data and could be used to predict the motion of all matter.

In the area of happiness, we are now in a situation similar to the state of affairs at the time of Brahe and Kepler. Psychologists have done a lot to gather measurements and data on happiness. But accumulating data is not sufficient if we lack a set of rules that organizes most of this information. Much like Newton's laws of motion, we need laws of happiness that illuminate what makes us happy.

True, emotions and states of mind are complex, but in Newton's day that's how people felt about the planets and the stars. Science is about peeling the artichoke of complexity, and getting to the core of the phenomenon by reducing that complexity.

Our quest for the first law of happiness begins with a simple question. What triggers happiness? Let's carefully consider the map of human emotions and ask: what is the basic mechanism that triggers many of our emotions?

Here is a true story from one of our students in a decision-making class: His seventeen-year-old daughter came home one day with her final grade for the year. She had scored an eight out of ten, which is very good, but still she wouldn't stop crying. When he asked her why, she answered: "My friends all got nine and nine and a half."

Without further ado, here is what we think is the first and most fundamental law of happiness.

> *The First Law—Comparison: Happiness (and unhappiness) is triggered by comparison.*

A comparison necessarily involves two objects. When it comes to happiness, the first of the two objects is the external reality and the second object is an expectation, a reference for comparison, that we judge against this reality. In the story of the student's daughter, the expectation is based on the scores of the friends. If her friends had scored seven instead of nine, then she would have been really happy with the very same score.

Putting it in simple and familiar terms,

HAPPINESS *equals* REALITY *minus* EXPECTATIONS

What we have just written is what we call the fundamental equation of happiness. Throughout this book, as new laws of happiness are introduced we will modify and enrich this fundamental law to make it more accurate and applicable to a wide range of life situations. The process of constructing the fundamental equation of happiness, together with exploring its implications, is the spinal cord of the book.

Comparison is the mechanism our mind uses to deal with the world. We judge performance of sports teams, companies, and students by means of relative judgments. By having references and creating expectations, our mind saves a lot of processing cost. By and large, most of the reality we process every day is in line with our expectations: the car is parked where we expected, the kitchen utensils are where they are supposed to be, the traffic lights work as expected, and so on. Thus, we live in a reality that is mostly familiar, allowing our minds to hum along comfortably in a world with few surprises. When references are unavailable or are too distant, reality becomes unfamiliar and we get confused, until the mind manages to set new frames of reference.

When our reality is not as we expect it to be, our emotions are activated. If the differences go into a positive direction, the mind enjoys the route and has a good time processing them, producing positive feelings of joy, pride, comfort, and pleasure. For example, if your flight arrives earlier than expected, you will be happy. On the other hand, if the flight is late, your reality is less desirable than your expectation and the mind produces negative feelings of annoyance.

For each thing that we possess and use, for each activity we do, our mind triggers positive and negative emotions based on how it compares to some expectation. If the expectation is relatively close to the pieces of reality that we observe, the mind needs to process only a few, minor differences. For example, if you live in suburban New York and move to suburban Connecticut, you need to adapt to only a few things since your new reality in general is somewhat similar to your old one. If the differences are too large, then the mind can no longer quickly process the comparisons and enters into confusion, until the new references are set. For example, moving from New York to India might cause much more stress than moving to Connecticut, since most of the realities you encounter will be quite different from your expectations (now you must adapt to different weather and a different language, for example). Likewise, if you are used to driving a car in which the steering wheel is on the left side, moving to England and having to drive on the right side of the car will be a challenge.

We need reference points to make sense of all that we observe. We require some preconceived image, called an *expectation* or *reference*, to help fill in the disparate pieces of information we encounter. This need is so strong that, in fact, what we perceive as the "objective" reality is itself a mixture of what is really out there and what we expect to see. Magicians take full advantage of our bias toward believing that what we see is what we expect to be there, not what is actually there.

What determines expectations? There are three key determinants of expectations. Let's explore the first of them in this chapter, the second one in the next chapter, and leave the third one for later.

EXPECTATIONS BASED ON SOCIAL COMPARISON

One factor that determines our expectations is what others in our peer group have, known as the "social comparison level." When we think about expectations this way, we get a possible equation for determining our happiness:

HAPPINESS *equals* WHAT I GET *minus* WHAT OTHERS GET

It is our human tendency to try to feel superior to others. Consider the following experiment, in which students at the Harvard School of Public Health were asked to choose in which of two worlds they would prefer to live.[2] In World A, your current yearly income is $50,000, and others earn $25,000. In World B, your current yearly income is $100,000, and others earn $200,000.

Which one would you choose?

A majority of the students preferred World A in spite of it providing half the income available in World B, presumably because their relative income position was higher. This same answer pattern was given for several other domains of life, such as intelligence and attractiveness. Again, people prefer lower absolute levels as long as they have an advantageous relative standing.

We compare ourselves with others perhaps more than what we would like to admit. Do we compare ourselves with the rich and famous? Or do we compare ourselves with our colleagues and relatives? In a classic study in *The American Soldier: Adjustment during Army Life*, satisfaction with promotion was higher in the military police unit where promotion chances were low. In the Air Force unit, where promotion chances were high, satisfaction was lower. This was due to the prevalence of Air Force personnel who felt entitled to a promotion; those in the military police, in contrast, saw promotion as an achievement and an accolade for good work.

This research shows that social comparison, like any comparison, is driven by the principle of similarity. People are likely to compare themselves to those who are similar in income and status. Even though our society is always looking up to the very rich and famous, and media communication sources are flooded with news of the latest popular singer, model, or social figure, when it comes to comparing ourselves to others we naturally carefully observe who is right next to us. Therefore, as much as we idolize Julia Roberts or Brad Pitt, when it comes to comparing, we will look at the Mary or Paul next door. A university professor is unlikely to compare herself to a movie star or a homeless person. She will most likely compare her lifestyle to those of other professors at her university and similarly situated colleagues at other comparable universities.

Even gods are not exempt from social comparison. Do you know how spiders came into existence? According to ancient Greek mythology, the goddess Minerva was a weaver. Her work was fine and beautiful. A peasant girl named Arachne was also an acclaimed weaver. Minerva challenged her to a contest, and both produced magnificent threads and the result was a tie. Minerva in a fury beat up and disgraced Arachne. Arachne was so despondent that she killed herself. Goddess Minerva then felt sorry and sprinkled Arachne's body with a magic liquid. Arachne was transformed into a spider with a gift for weaving like no other.

Our relative social position not only results in comparisons with others, but also can have real biological consequences. One study found that dominant vervet monkeys had higher levels of the neurotransmitter serotonin, which is associated with enhanced feelings of well-being, than did subordinate monkeys. Curiously, when the dominant monkey was removed from the group, its serotonin levels decreased, and when a new monkey became dominant, its levels increased.[3] These findings suggest that our happiness, even at a biological level, is closely dependent on our status relative to others. Apparently, it really is difficult, but by no means impossible, to simply be happy with what we have.

THE PURPOSE OF SOCIAL COMPARISON

Hyperion is the world's tallest tree, at about 380 feet, and there are more than one hundred other redwood trees in forests throughout Northern California that are about as tall as a football field is long. Why do redwood trees grow so tall? It is because if these trees have the right climate and soil, then the only limiting factor is sunlight. Many young trees wither and die in the shade produced by larger trees. When an old tree dies and falls down, a ring of new trees springs to life and each grows rapidly vying for the light. Trees do not compete consciously and cannot willfully choose to be half as tall in order to conserve energy; however, the same design of nature that kills uncountable seedlings has produced every single surviving tree in the ancient forest in California, all of which are more than four thousand years old.

In the early stages of human development, the physically strongest men succeeded best as hunter-gatherers and, subsequently, in securing mates and thus transferring their brute physical characteristics to successive generations. When humans discovered agriculture, food sources became more stable and the population increased, which inevitably led to competition for resources. Gradually, the evolutionary advantage shifted to those who were more inventive in developing and using the best weapons or traps and who were more cunning in warfare. Therefore, competition for resources explains very well why social comparison is so ingrained.

Once the basic needs of food, shelter, and good health are met, there are no significant survival advantages to having greater material possessions. Why, then, are we not content and happy? The social psychologist

Leon Festinger observed that we use social comparisons as a means by which we determine how well we are doing.[4] Could it be that our discontent is rooted in the fact that we constantly make social comparisons between ourselves and our peers in terms of wealth and status, as a yardstick of success and self-worth?

TAMING COMPARISONS

> Don't worry about being better than somebody else, but never cease trying to be the best you can be. You have control over that, not the other.
> —John Wooden, legendary basketball coach

Coach Wooden's advice is clearly based on an understanding of the powerful need we all have to compare ourselves with others, and of how important it is to turn our focus inward. He emphasizes that our success is not relative to that of others. He believed that if you make the effort to become the best you are capable of becoming, then you will have self-satisfaction and achieve peace of mind. On the other hand, if you continue to engage in social comparison, not only are you likely to neglect your self-improvement, but you risk succumbing to the crippling emotions of envy and hatred.

Envy and hatred are universal emotions, and are persistent obstacles to happiness. There's a reason why literary work has always embraced their dramatic tension. For example, the *Mahabharata*—the longest epic poem ever written—shows how envy caused the downfall of a great kingdom.

Set in ancient India, the *Mahabharata* tells the story of the Kauravas, the sons of a king, and the Pandavas, the sons of his brother. These two branches of the same family were bitter rivals. Despite the Kauravas' mischief and attempts to destroy the Pandavas, a peace was reached when the kingdom was divided, with the Kauravas ruling one part and the Pandavas ruling the other. The Kauravas, nevertheless, still envied the Pandavas and devised a scheme to destroy them. They invited the

Pandavas to a rigged game of dice in which they cheated to win all of the Pandavas' property. The Pandavas lost and were exiled from the kingdom for twelve years, with the further condition that they spend a thirteenth year incognito, during which the exile would begin again if they were spotted or recognized. The Pandavas fulfilled these conditions, but the Kauravas still refused to share the kingdom with them. A bloody war ensued. The Pandavas won the war at the cost of a massive slaughter of family and friends on both sides. This was a pyrrhic victory for the Pandavas, who went on to rule a devastated kingdom.

As with the warring factions in the *Mahabharata,* envy and social comparison can lead any of us to overlook the good things we have in a futile attempt to gain something more. In your career, you may believe that the nature of business and the competitive success it requires makes social comparisons unavoidable. You may also think that stepping out of the business world would allow you to avoid making money-related comparisons and to experience less envy. It is inevitable to make comparisons in all facets of life. Not even monks, poets, or priests can be free from such comparisons.

We believe that no amount of success can increase happiness if social comparisons remain unchecked. This is because expectations keep rising. When you increase your wealth or status, you'll then compare yourself to more prosperous peers, and your sense of relative wealth and status will remain the same. Bertrand Russell put it well in *The Conquest of Happiness:* "If you desire glory, you may envy Napoleon. But Napoleon envied Cesar, Cesar envied Alexander, and Alexander, I dare say, envied Hercules, who never existed."[5]

You might ask yourself, can't we just compare ourselves to those less fortunate than we are and thus improve our happiness by this self-serving social comparison? Of course you can, with the expected results. For example, in a study titled "When Less Is More: Counterfactual Thinking and Satisfaction among Olympic Medalists," Tom Gilovich and his colleagues found that Olympic bronze medalists are actually happier than silver medalists. The silver medalists regret coming so close but not winning, whereas the bronze medalists compare them-selves with the entire field and are thrilled to have won a medal at all.[6]

A SMART APPROACH TO SOCIAL COMPARISONS

Social comparisons influence our expectations at a mostly unconscious level, which explains why the "peer pressure" effect is so pervasive and lasting. It's something we never completely outgrow. And the more sim-ilar our peers are to us in terms of age, education, and income, the more their behavior will influence our own.

Since most of this social comparison is unconscious, simply recog-nizing that we do it at all can help limit its impact. You could also recog-nize that, just as others influence you, you influence them as well. Here are four strategies to help deal with our natural tendency to compare ourselves with others:

1. *Choose the Right Pond.* That is, be aware of your capacities and limitations, and choose social groups that are a good fit for you. A talented journalist will be happy if her peers respect her, but if she gives up her career as a journalist and becomes a stockbroker with a much higher salary, her happiness may actually decline. This is because her new peer group is now other stockbrokers, who may be earning even more. Simply put, pay attention to how your choices will affect to whom you compare yourself.

2. *Selective Comparison.* That is, compare yourself to others only on dimensions that favor you. If a neighbor's new BMW or swimming pool is making you envious, you can take delight in your better health or availability of more free time to spend with family and friends. If we feel secure in our devotion to a hobby, social service, or religion, then the advantages of the neighbor on some material dimension may seem less important. It is easy to compare what we have to others in a peer group on conspicuous and easily observed dimensions. So, we must

develop mental discipline in taking a broader perspective on life and in consciously looking for reasons to be grateful about our own situation.

3. *Acts of Kindness.* Helping others who are less fortunate is satisfying on its own. Through these acts of kindness we can develop relationships with others who are in greater need and thus feel more secure in our own endowment. Each of us is unique and has the capacity to appreciate our own good fortune. It has been found that through mood induction, children can be made more generous to poor kids.[7] With such training of mind, envy becomes a fleeting thought rather than a persistent mental condition.

4. *Cultivate an Attitude of Admiration.* Admiration is an antidote for envy. Don't you know people who feel genuinely happy when you tell them about some good fortune that has come your way (a promotion, your child's success in school)? Such people have learned to appreciate others' good fortune and rejoice in their success. Everyone has the capacity to enjoy their neighbor's garden without diminishing the joy their own garden brings them; in fact, your joy is doubled if you are able to learn this way of looking at situations.

. . .

MUDITA—AN ENDLESS WELLSPRING OF HAPPINESS

Although we may not want to admit it, we often take delight in the misfortunes of others. The Germans call this *Schadenfreude*, a word now made popular through a song in the musical *Avenue Q.* For example, we may laugh at the pratfalls of a circus clown or enjoy that the former high school cheerleader whom everyone envied hasn't aged well. Schadenfreude is basically a particular type of social comparison that we use to make us feel better about ourselves. But do these thoughts really make us happy?

At its core, schadenfreude is really just a form of envy and resentment that works out in our favor this time. Taken to its extreme, an obsessive desire to find joy in the misfortune of others is toxic to happiness.

But, just as we all harbor a tendency to engage in schadenfreude, we are also all capable of the opposite tendency: *mudita*, the Buddhist concept of taking pleasure in the successes of others. As with schadenfreude, we are all familiar with mudita, as when we celebrate the successes of close friends and family. What most of us fail to realize is that the more we can cultivate mudita toward a larger universe of people, the greater our own happiness can be.

It is not easy to genuinely experience mudita, but if you take a moment to think about the people whose success you do celebrate—not just family and friends, but also celebrities, athletes, and many others you've never met—you realize that the list is longer than you thought.

Now that you realize mudita is a bigger part of your life than you realized, you could work to experience it even more often. There is virtually an endless list of people whose accomplishments could bring you joy. As many Buddhist teachings espouse, mudita represents an infinite wellspring of joy that is available to any of us at any point in our lives. All we need to do to bring that joy into our lives is to diminish the negative effects of social comparison (envy, jealousy, shame, and sadness) and to cultivate the positive effects (admiration, love, and joy).

HAPPINESS IN ACTION

Each day take joy in someone else's success or good fortune. This person could be a colleague at work, a family member, or even a person in the news. To make this process easier, imagine that this person is just like someone you know and love. As you continue this practice, you'll find it easier and easier to find joy and happiness in other people's successes.

CHAPTER 4

The Second Law of Happiness

Motion of Expectation

> It is not the strongest of species that survive, or the most
> intelligent, but the one most responsive to change.
> —Charles Darwin

Expectations play a key role in the laws of happiness. But what determines our expectations? We have argued that what others have influences our expectations. But social comparison is just one of three main
factors that influence expectations. What is the second main factor?

Here is one simple but powerful experiment. Take three glasses. Fill
one glass with hot water (not hot enough to hurt your hand), one with
ice water (take the ice out before you begin), and one with water that is
room temperature. Next, put one finger of your right hand in the hot
water and one finger of your left hand in the cold water. Keep them in
the water for about one minute. Then, put both fingers in the room
temperature water. What do you experience?

Well, the finger that used to be in hot water got adapted to hot and
now feels the room temperature water as cold. And the finger that used
to be in ice cold water got adapted to cold and now feels the room temperature water as hot. Here is the magic: the same reality produces different experiences because of adaptation. The environment, in this case
the temperature, has changed the reference of comparison and what
before used to be lukewarm water is now experienced as hot or cold,

depending on the new reference. What you perceive is not the stimulus per se, but the difference between the current stimulation and the past stimulation.[1] In other words, what you have experienced in the *past* influences your expectations.

REALITY AND EXPECTATIONS

Few people are like Miss Havisham in Charles Dickens's *Great Expectations,* who lives a life stopped in time after her wedding is canceled. Most people adjust to a new reality both in good times (upward adjustment) and in bad times (downward adjustment), such that whatever the reality becomes it eventually begins to feel normal. One important quality of references and expectations is that they move in the direction of the current reality. Because expectations are fundamental to understanding happiness, the fact that they move deserves to be a law:

> *The Second Law—Motion of Expectations: Expectations change, always moving toward the new reality.*

As students, most of us live in a small apartment (or a dormitory room) with roommates, drive an old car, and eat in inexpensive restaurants. But we are happy, as our expectations are low. Upon getting a job, we may live in a condominium, drive a new car, and eat in relatively more expensive restaurants. Are we happier? As our income gradually increases, expectations also increase. So the reality is higher, but expectations are also higher, and we are now settled into a lifestyle that may require independent living, a better car, and dining in fancier restaurants.

As students, our expectations were also influenced by the lifestyles of the people in our peer group, who were also students. After graduation, the peer group shifted to higher earning coworkers. If everyone else in the office is driving a late-model German sedan, then your old junker is suddenly much less satisfying than it was on campus.

Based on the previous examples, we can see that there are two basic ways in which expectations change: either we adapt, so that our expectations are simply what we're used to, or we compare ourselves with others, so that we expect to get what our peers have.

EXPECTATIONS CHANGE BY ADAPTATION

Simply put, what you got in the past can determine your expectations for the future. You experienced this by placing your fingers in hot and cold water. Each finger "expected" to remain either hot or cold, but when they were placed in room temperature water, the expectation was no longer met and the hot finger felt cold while the cold finger felt hot.

To frame it as an equation, this change of expectations by adaptation suggests that:

HAPPINESS *equals*
WHAT I GET TODAY *minus* WHAT I GOT IN THE PAST

Who among us hasn't dreamed of improving some part of our lives in the hopes of achieving lasting happiness? Whether it's more money or a better love life, it's natural to believe that if we just had a little bit more we'd be so much happier from now on. But when we try to make our reality better than our expectation in order to obtain happiness, a curious side effect occurs: our expectations rise as well! As expectations get closer and closer to reality, our happiness levels revert to a neutral level, and we find we're just as happy (or unhappy) as we were before.

The neuroscientist Wolfram Schultz found that even monkeys exhibit this kind of adaptation. He found that when monkeys were given a treat of raisins rather than their customary apples, they showed a big jump in activity in the reward centers of their brains. Over time, though, that activity diminished as the monkeys adapted to their new food. When the monkeys were once again given apples, they showed disappointment at first, but eventually they adjusted and their brain activity returned to where it was before they were ever given the raisins.[2]

In the 1970s, the researchers Philip Brickman and Donald Campbell coined a term for this phenomenon, the *hedonic treadmill,* suggesting that good things make us only temporarily happy and bad things make us only temporarily unhappy. This term defines our ability to quickly adapt to good things by taking them for granted. If adaptation to things (cars, watches, electronics) is so quick, why do we desire new models so intensely that we cannot wait to return to the car dealership or the shopping mall? Our prediction of how much we will enjoy the new car is heavily biased by the thought of happiness we will experience when we first drive the car home from the dealership. We may not necessarily get the same happiness boost for the next few years when the car will be parked in our garage while we drool over pictures of the newest model.

That is because our mind does not anticipate adaptation, and we cannot see that our future basis for comparison will be different from the current one. As you accumulate goods, experiences, and victories, your expectations also rise. Therefore, having more today is perceived as always preferable, but when we get used to having more, we need to have even more still, and we're then stuck on the treadmill.

Stop for a minute and think about the movements of your arms and legs, and how crucial it is to your life that you can move around without the need of a wheelchair. What if suddenly you couldn't walk? Think about your vision as you read this book; how much different would your life be if you suddenly went blind? It would be a monumental undertaking to adjust to your new life. Now suppose you sought advice from someone who was born blind or unable to walk. While they could certainly relate to the challenges you face, they would likely not share your profound despair, having never known a life of sight or mobility. Simply put, they're not likely to miss what they never had.

The same pattern tends to affect lifestyle and income. One tragic example that illustrated this point is the case of German billionaire Adolf Merckle, who committed suicide in 2009 in the wake of financial problems. Even after a decline in his fortune, Merckle remained one of the richest men on Earth. It was not his absolute wealth but its precipitous decline, as well as the resulting loss of pride and prestige, that caused him to take his life.

To illustrate the impact of adaptation under more mundane conditions, let's look at the following group of people. Anne is originally from a low-income family, but through hard work she managed to attend a university and earn a degree, which has enabled her to get a good job. Her work performance improves over time as she learns how to better manage her tasks. Anne's monthly salary started at $1,000 and increased to $2,000.

Bill was brought up in a middle-class community and has been able to afford the same living standard his entire life. He is on a stable career path and his income is unlikely to change very much. Bill's monthly salary will probably stay at a constant level of $2,000.

Carol was a very wealthy individual who experienced a steady decline in her income due to a sequence of misfortunes in her family business. She is still able to afford a decent house in an upper middle-class neighborhood, but she had to sell her spectacular beach house. Carol's monthly income started at $3,000 and has steadily declined to $2,000.

Let's assume that these three characters don't know one another, so there is no social comparison taking place among them. They all have sufficient budget to cover their basic needs, which we'll assume total about $1,000 per month. Who would you say is the happiest person? Who would you rather be: Anne, Bill, or Carol?

If we ask an economist from the old school, he would argue, quite convincingly, that these income profiles follow a "dominance relationship." Carol's income, which moves between $3,000 and $2,000, is higher, period after period, than Bill's income, which is $2,000. Hence, Carol must be happier than Bill. By the same logic, Bill's income is higher than Anne's, which moves between $1,000 and $2,000. If money can indeed buy happiness, then the prediction is simple: Carol is the happiest, followed by Bill, and then Anne.

What is your prediction? Perhaps you said that Anne is the happiest. If so, then your prediction agrees with what our laws of happiness say as well. Anne, who experienced an increase in monthly income of $1,000, should be happiest, followed by Bill, whose income has remained constant over time. In turn, Bill is probably happier than Carol, whose monthly income has declined by $1,000.

Of course, this does not imply that people with less money are happier, but that people *with more money than they had before* should be happier. This crescendo effect (less to more) as a determinant of happiness is a key implication of our laws of happiness.

·   ·   ·

We surveyed 103 people from Spain. In one of our questions, we asked them to rank the happiness of Anne, Bill, and Carol. Not surprisingly, most people predicted that Anne, whose income started low and increased over time, would be the happiest. Carol, whose income was substantially higher than that of Anne, but declined over time, was predicted to be the least happy. People intuitively recognize that an increasing sequence of income, less to more, is more important than the absolute level of income.

·   ·   ·

ADAPTATION TO LIFE CIRCUMSTANCES

The summary of the first two laws of happiness is condensed in the following equation:

HAPPINESS *equals*
REALITY *minus* SHIFTING EXPECTATIONS

and expectations shift based on adaptation to our past living standards and social comparison, that is

EXPECTATIONS SHIFT *depending on*
WHAT I GOT IN THE PAST *and* WHAT OTHERS GET

To show how expectations shift depending on what I got in the past (adaptation) and what the others get (social comparison), let's take the example of a golf player. Jim is a novice player who, together with a group of friends, started playing golf recently. What determines the quality of his golf experience? If his score today is better than both his past performance and that of his friends, then he will surely feel happy. Of course, if Jim scores worse than usual and worse than his friends, then he will feel miserable. What if he scores better than his usual, but worse than his friends? Then, he will have mixed feelings. Perhaps he will be able to focus on positive comparisons with his past, but the fact that he has done worse than his friends will take some of the happiness out of his day. The same mixed feelings, alternation between positive and negative emotions, will happen if Jim does better than his friends but worse than his usual performance.

Since farming was invented ten thousand years ago, humans have gone from living in huts to living in houses, from walking miles to driving cars, and from taking the entire day to hunt for food to microwaving it in a matter of seconds. Over time, humans have also adapted to diseases and genetic resistance has even appeared in some populations. It is amazing how highly adaptive we are, and this adaptability has helped us survive climate changes, diseases, and wars. But as we will show, this is also the reason why we are never satisfied for long when good fortune does come our way.

The modern version of this process can be illustrated by the following hypothetical situation. You are quite content living in your neighborhood, but unexpectedly you receive a job offer with much higher pay. You now decide to move to a more prosperous neighborhood. Are you happier? You are delighted in the beginning, but soon you get used to the comforts of your new life and your nicer surroundings and you start to eye neighbors who have fancier cars or houses. The very same cycle preys on our happiness as our living standard and peer group comparison keeps changing.

Adaptation is easy to grasp intuitively. We all have experienced the uplift of some new possession, only to have that elation diminish over time. Similarly, we may have experienced that the pain of some negative event has faded over time.

PARTIAL ADAPTATION

Adaptation tempers our happiness both in good times and in bad times. Is adaptation total and complete, or just partial? As an example, meet Abe, Beth, and Chris. They live in a small town where the average annual income is $50,000. For a long time, Abe, Beth, and Chris all had this average income of $50,000, which would cover their annual expenses. Suddenly, Abe gets a promotion, with a salary increase of $10,000. Beth maintains her salary, while Chris has to switch jobs and accept a salary reduction of $10,000. After this change, Abe, Beth, and Chris's salaries remain constant at this new level of $60,000, $50,000, and $40,000, respectively.

What would you predict to be the happiness seismogram of these three individuals over the next months? After sufficient time has passed, will their happiness revert to the same level as it was before the shift? Suppose that they do not know each other, but they may compare their own circumstances with the town's average salary of $50,000.

Before the change in salary, Abe, Beth, and Chris were equally happy. At the moment of the increase, Abe will experience a sudden increase in happiness, due to his larger salary. In the case of *full adaptation,* the increase will fade away little by little as he adapts to the new income level. Beth's happiness seismogram will remain flat, as her situation doesn't change. Chris, by comparison, will experience severe unhappiness due to his loss in income. Over time, however, he will also revert to his old level of happiness as he adapts to a more frugal life.

Bernard Van Praag and Ada Ferrer-i-Carbonell are two economists from Erasmus University and the Institute for Economic Analysis. They have carefully studied how factors such as absolute income, relative income, health, marriage, job, and even noise affect life satisfaction. In particular, they have studied the effect that a permanent change in income has on happiness. Their conclusion is that an increase in salary does translate into an increase in life satisfaction. As predicted by adaptation, most of this increase in happiness is transitory. However, a small part of the increase is permanent. In other words, rather than full adaptation we have *partial adaptation*.

Indeed, using large data samples, these two economists estimate that, of the happiness increase initially experienced, 80 percent of it is transitory, and 20 percent is permanent. The permanent effect is due to the nonadaptive aspects of some of the goods we purchase and some permanent effects of the improvement in social comparison. So, at least according to these data, money *can* buy happiness, but it usually doesn't buy as much as we expect.

Partial adaptation has also been found on losses, with about 80 percent of the initial unhappiness fading over time. Van Praag and Ferrer-i-Carbonell find that losses are felt more intensely than gains, reflecting that "the income gap causes the individual more pain if he or she is on the wrong side, whilst a positive gap is a cause for less celebration if one is on the right side."[3] We will explore this asymmetry between gains and losses in the next chapter, through the third law of happiness.

. . .

GETTING THE "GOODS" ON HAPPINESS

It is important to recognize that we don't adapt to every possession or experience to the same degree. Some things lose their luster immediately after we get them, whereas others maintain their appeal forever. One practical implication of our laws of happiness, which will unfold in subsequent chapters, is the classification of goods and activities into five different types. Throughout the book, we will use the terms *goods* and *activities* interchangeably. *Goods* emphasizes consumption and the use of money, whereas *activities* emphasizes the use of time.

Goods and activities are the "reality" part of our fundamental equation. Understanding the distinctions among different types of goods, as we'll call them, can help us to be more realistic in forecasting happiness and protect us against future disappointments. Let's introduce a key distinction between two types of goods, the basic and the adaptive. The three additional types of goods will be discussed in later chapters.

Basic Goods

In the Harvard study on social comparison that we saw in the previous chapter, most respondents cared about their relative income rather than their absolute income. In this same study, the same question was asked, but using health and vacation, rather than income, in the question. Students preferred the option with a greater absolute number of vacation days for themselves even though others had even more vacation days. This world was preferred to a world where they had fewer vacation days in absolute terms but more days relative to the peers. Similarly, people prefer to be happily married for a longer period of time even if their peers have been happily married longer than themselves. In these domains, people do not exhibit a bias for relative advantage; thus, their happiness depends on the absolute levels of outcome received and is less contingent on the outcomes of others.

Thus, there are some goods and experiences we hardly adapt to at all. The pleasure we derive from them remains more or less constant. We call these basic goods, and they include food, rest, sex, health, exercise, or socializing with friends and family. The existence of these basic goods explains the 20 percent permanent increase of happiness after a permanent income increase.

We always appreciate a hearty meal when we're hungry or a good night's sleep when we're tired. Basic goods, by definition, are those for which our adaptation level changes little, if at all. We could also call them nonadaptive goods, or absolute goods.

Adaptive Goods

The happiness derived from adaptive goods wears off quickly. After your first experience with an adaptive good, such as the comfort of new furniture, the wizardry of electronic gadgets, or the feel of better clothes or jewelry, you have to keep on consuming at the same level if you want to sustain the same degree of happiness you had when you started. We often fail to anticipate what our expectations will be in the future, and miscalculate how happy we will be.

We often confuse adaptive goods with basic goods and believe that the pleasure we derive from them will remain constant. But, as we all know, the thrill of driving that new car fades and we find ourselves back where we started. The same thing happens with comfort, electronic gadgets, and higher-quality clothes and jewelry. Of course, all these goods have some basic features, and that is why adaptation is only partial, and some permanent happiness remains after purchasing these goods.

Understanding the difference between basic and adaptive goods is one key to maximizing happiness. To the extent that we can appreciate and enjoy our basic goods while recognizing and anticipating the diminishing returns we'll receive from our adaptive goods, we'll be better positioned to achieve greater happiness.

So, you should try to appreciate that small ice cream cone on a hot day, and recognize the satisfaction you derive from a pleasant lunch with a friend or vacationing in a new place. You can count on these experiences and always enjoy them. As for the adaptive goods, it's important that you consume them in a smart way, knowing that their positive impact will diminish over time.

Later in the book we will explain exactly how to deal with these different types of goods—as well as "cumulative goods," which are adaptive goods that can behave like basic goods—to increase happiness. For now, though, just understanding the differences between them is a big step in the right direction.

We hope that we have convinced you that expectations change by adaptation to our past and the behavior of our peer group. These two principles of the Law of Motion of Expectations—adaptation and social comparison—are fundamental to understanding how to maximize happiness in your life. A third way in which expectations can change is by purposefully finding new ways to see reality. Later, we devote a whole chapter to reframing activities, to explore this third way to influence expectations.

. . .

HAPPINESS IN ACTION

Take a moment to think about just how satisfied you are with your life as a whole. Rate your level of happiness on a scale from 1 to 10, with 1 meaning "extremely unhappy" and 10 meaning "extremely happy."

Then, think about one way that you could increase your happiness without buying or experiencing something you think you want. So, for example, rather than thinking that owning a new flat-screen HDTV would make you happier, think about how you could become more satisfied with your current TV. Or, rather than wishing you had more money, think about how much you enjoy the things you have or think about the priceless goods or experiences that enrich your life.

CHAPTER 5

The Third Law of Happiness

Aversion to Loss

The dread of evil is a much more forcible principle of human
actions than the prospect of good.
—John Locke

Let's imagine a game. Toss a coin in the air. If the coin lands on tails, you
lose ten dollars; but, if the coin lands on heads, you win some amount
of money. What is the minimum amount that you would have to win
for you to play the game? The odds of the coin landing on heads or tails
are equal, so it would be fair to suggest that you should stand to win the
same amount that you could lose, ten dollars. But in this case, most of us
don't want to play fair. In fact, most people feel that to compensate for
the potential loss of ten dollars, the potential winnings should be about
twenty-five dollars.

The unhappiness experienced from a loss of ten dollars is significantly more intense than the happiness experienced from a gain of ten
dollars. Recall that happydons is our unit of measurement of happiness, which accounts for the intensity and duration of positive and negative emotions. Using our units of measurement, if a loss of ten dollars
produces -5 happydons, then a gain of ten dollars produces much less
(say, $+2$ happydons). In this example, it is a gain of twenty-five dollars that produces 5 happydons, and hence compensates for the loss.
The ratio of intensity between losses and gains is called the coefficient

of loss aversion, and the average is approximately 2.5. Of course, some of us are aggressive gamblers and some of us are quite conservative, so the coefficient of loss aversion can vary greatly depending on the person and circumstance. Nonetheless, this tendency to weigh losses greater than gains is widespread, and leads us to the third law of happiness:

The Third Law—Aversion to Loss: Losses are felt more keenly than equivalent gains.

This law is called the Law of Hedonic Asymmetry by the Dutch psychologist Nico Frijda,[1] or Loss Aversion by Kahneman and Tversky. According to the Law of Aversion to Loss, a ten dollar gain yields +2 happydons, but a ten dollar loss robs us of 5 happydons.

In the absence of loss aversion, the equation "Happiness is reality minus expectations" can be plotted on a graph, where the horizontal axis measures reality and the vertical axis indicates the happiness associated with that reality, measured in happydons. On the horizontal axis, first mark the point where the expectations are. Now draw a straight and increasing line with the only condition that the line has to cross the horizontal axis at the point were you marked the level of expectations. On the vertical axis, that crossing point corresponds to zero happiness. Hence, reality below expectations yields unhappiness, and reality above expectations yields happiness. The slope of the line can be chosen arbitrarily, as we can scale the happiness the way we want.

To account for loss aversion, simply break the straight line as if it were a bread stick. Keep the positive portion the same, and increase the slope of the negative portion, making it at least twice as steep as the positive portion (see figure 4). Plainly, the line measuring unhappiness is steeper than the line measuring happiness. Thus, we tend to become unhappy more easily, more quickly, and more severely than we become happy.

Loss aversion is universal. Football coaches, poker players, and deal makers all know that the pain from a loss tends to be felt more strongly than the joy from a win.

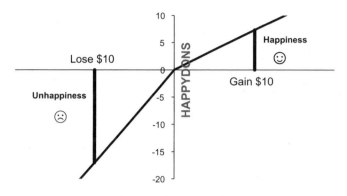

Figure 4. Loss Aversion

WHAT IS A LOSS?

Suppose everyone in your department gets a 5 percent pay cut, which is necessary to avoid layoffs. But you receive only a 3 percent pay cut. Surely, your take-home pay is now lower than what it was before the pay cut, but don't you feel a bit of satisfaction that you were spared the full 5 percent pay cut? Whether an outcome is perceived as a gain or a loss depends on the reference level.

REALITY *better than* EXPECTATIONS *equals* GAIN

REALITY *worse than* EXPECTATIONS *equals* LOSS

Suppose you bought a plane ticket from Los Angeles to San Francisco for $89. You feel good about your purchase, as the regular price for the same ticket is $154. But as you strike up a conversation with a fellow passenger, you find out that he bought his ticket for only $49. Suddenly, your $89 ticket doesn't seem like such a good deal. What happened is that the zero of your happiness curve shifted from the original price of $154 to the new reference price of $49 that the guy sitting next to you paid. Originally, you were on the happiness side of the curve, since you paid less than your reference price of $154. But with the new information, your reference level shifted to $49; and with respect to the new curve, your purchase price of $89 is in the unhappiness region. So, the same purchase price of $89 yields moderate happiness when compared to the regular price of $154, but more severe unhappiness when compared to the $49 price paid by your new buddy.

The Yale psychology professor Laurie Santos ran a study where capuchin monkeys were offered pieces of apple in exchange for tokens.[2] One person would offer a single piece of apple, but when the monkey paid with the token, it actually received two pieces of apple. Another person offered three pieces of apple, but gave only two in exchange for the token. Santos found that the monkeys preferred to deal with the first person rather than the second, even though they received two pieces of apple either way. So, even nonhuman primates perform comparisons and are averse to losses.

If we could just pick reference points that put us on the happiness side of the curve, we would be more likely to feel happy. But, as suggested by the behavior of our capuchin cousins, we may just be hardwired to do the exact opposite.

In industrialized societies, we seem much more inclined to try to shift our reality by striving to make more money, moving to a new location, buying a new electronic gadget, and so forth. But a change in reality often causes expectations to change as well, leaving us no happier than we were before.

THE POWER OF LOSS AVERSION

Do you know how to use loss aversion to influence choices and behavior for the best? The Yale professors Ian Ayres and Dean Karlan have devised a system to facilitate achievement of personal goals such as weight loss or quit smoking. The system is based on the idea that people will try a lot harder to avoid losing five hundred dollars than they will to gain five hundred dollars. So, at the start of your diet you would deposit five hundred dollars in an escrow account. If you meet your weight-loss goal, then the money is returned to you; however, if you fail to meet your goal, the money is given to charity.[3]

In the Philippines, a savings account arrangement was used to help people quit smoking. The smokers put their cigarette money into a bank account. At the end of six months, if tests revealed nicotine in their systems, the money was given to charity. The program was a huge success, as people did not want to lose their savings. As these examples clearly illustrate, framing something as a loss is a powerful motivator to help us change our behavior.

Let us take another example where the same reality could produce a feeling of either a gain or a loss. Suppose you are about to pump gas into your vehicle. At one pump, there is a sign that says:

> The price is $3.15 per gallon. There is a 15 cent extra charge for those paying with credit card.

At another pump, the sign says:

> The price is $3.30 per gallon. There is a 15 cent discount for those paying with cash.

Obviously, both signs are equivalent, boiling down to a cost of $3.30 per gallon if paid with credit card, and of $3.15 per gallon if paid with cash. However, the emotional reaction they trigger is very different. Which sign will affect your payment method the most? Which sign will make you happier, the one that charges 15 cents for credit cards, or the one that saves 15 cents for cash? When it comes to happiness, it is better to avoid losses. Therefore, most people pay in cash when they are told that the credit card has a surcharge. In response to the second sign, saving 15 cents if using cash, people are happy both paying with credit card (more convenient) or by cash (discounted price). Therefore, it has less influence on the decision, and produces more happiness.

Richard H. Thaler of the University of Chicago Booth School of Business has explored many ways in which loss aversion affects our lives, and how it can be used for good. He and Shlomo Benartzi of the UCLA

Anderson School of Management have successfully gotten employees to save more for retirement. Their program, Save More Tomorrow, is based on a simple idea: employees resist putting money in their pension plans because it reduces their monthly income and creates a feeling of loss. Instead, they propose that employees commit to a plan that adds a fraction of their future salary *increases* to the pension plan.[4] The plan has been very successful in increasing the savings of employees at many companies.

Loss aversion has implications for buying and selling decisions. Our valuation of objects depends, among many other circumstantial factors, on whether we possess the object or not. When the sunglasses are not ours, possessing them is seen as a gain, for which the most we are willing to pay is, say, fifty dollars. When the glasses are ours, then not having them is seen as a loss, and the least we are willing to accept to sell them would be around twice as much, 100 dollars. This is known as the *endowment effect*.

THE RAT RACE

In our decision analysis courses, we play a little game with the students. In this game, which economists like to call a "war of attrition," we auction off a five-dollar bill. Sounds like a rather mundane exercise, right? Well, there's a twist. In the auction, the highest bidder wins the five dollars. But both the highest and second-highest bidders have to pay up. Therefore, the winner's net profit is five dollars minus his bid, but the runner up loses his bid entirely.

We have been playing this game with our MBA students for years, and here's what almost always happens:

At first, the bidding very quickly approaches $5. For example, there will be a high bid of $4.50 and second highest bid of $4.00. Suddenly, the second highest bid is increased to $5.00 (to avoid losing his previous bid of $4.00). But then, the other contestant bids $5.50. It might at first glance seem ridiculous to bid more than the bill is actually worth, but the bidder would rather win the auction and lose just $.50, than come in second and lose $4.50. The game usually escalates to bids around $7.00 or $8.00, because nobody wants to lose. When it's all over, the "winner" of the auction is usually quite unhappy. After all, he paid $8.00 to own a five-dollar bill. The loser is even less happy, with a net loss of $7.00. What's there to celebrate?

The same happens when we get trapped in social comparison games in real life: Most of us will admit to deriving some pleasure from being the first among our friends to own the latest new gadget. But the happiness we derive from being first fades, while the premium we paid for the privilege is gone for good. In the end, we often find that fleeting happiness was just not worth the cost, but it's so enticing that it's difficult to resist.

HAPPINESS IN ACTION

When you go for an overseas trip, budget a fixed amount—say, one hundred dollars—to cover possible losses that you may experience during the trip. You will not feel so bad when you realize that a taxi driver overcharged you, or that the sunglasses are nowhere to be found. We all hate losing, but if we take a broader view, we can avoid the feeling of loss because expectations have been adjusted beforehand.

Similarly, at the beginning of the year, create a budget for unexpected financial losses such as a car repair, a broken glass, a parking ticket. Should any such losses occur, you will not feel so bad as long as you are within budget.

CHAPTER 6

The Fourth Law of Happiness

Diminishing Sensitivity

The quantity of happiness will not go on increasing in
anything near the same proportion as the quantity of wealth.
 —Jeremy Bentham

Compare the emotion of winning ten thousand dollars from a call-in
radio show with the emotion of winning one hundred thousand dollars
from the lottery. If what we have said before is true—that happiness
associated with gains is a straight line of reality minus expectations—
then the lottery ticket is supposed to give you ten times more happydons than the call-in radio prize does. Is this correct? Intuitively, we see
that we will be happier with the lottery windfall, but not ten times as
much. In other words, there is diminishing sensitivity to gains.

Happiness or unhappiness cannot be taken to blissful or tragic
extremes in a straightforward way. Basically, the linear relationship
between happiness and consumption over a reference level is an oversimplification. To make the relationship between reality and happiness

more accurate, we need to account for diminishing sensitivity. Diminishing sensitivity is the fourth law of happiness.

The Fourth Law—Diminishing Sensitivity: Happiness is not proportional to the difference between reality and expectation; rather, the increase in happiness slows as reality moves further from expectation.

The law of diminishing sensitivity simply says that doubling the stimulus does not double the intensity of the emotional response. For example, the first bite of ice cream on a hot day tastes delicious; the second bite tastes good, but a bit less so, and the third bite even less than the second. In fact, the ice cream remains tasty until you are finished, but the deliciousness perceived by us gradually diminishes.

THE HAPPINESS S-CURVE

Just as the third law of happiness showed us that the unhappiness side of the graph is steeper, the fourth law will take it one step further by adding curvature to these lines (see figure 5). In combination, our laws start with the basic equation:

HAPPINESS equals REALITY minus EXPECTATIONS

and transform it into the more accurate version:[1]

HAPPINESS is an S-curve of
REALITY minus SHIFTING EXPECTATIONS

We can still see that happiness increases less steeply than unhappiness, but now those increases lessen as reality moves further from expectations, and the graph levels off in both directions. So greater positive experiences create proportionately less happiness, and more severe negative experiences create proportionately less misery.

In every event we experience, our mind compares the reality we face with our expectations of the world. That is our first law. As we experience this event repeatedly, our lazy mind tries to minimize the

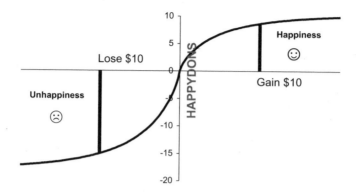

Figure 5. The Happiness S-Curve

difference between reality and expectations. Because expectations chase reality, we expect that on a typical day we will find few differences between reality and expectations. That is our second law. Negative comparisons reduce happiness at least twice as much as equivalent positive comparisons would increase happiness. This is our third law. In addition, happiness does not grow in proportion to the difference between reality and expectations. Instead, there is diminishing sensitivity to both large gains and large losses. This is our fourth law.

The four laws help us understand why we feel better or worse even though the reality remains the same. The S-curve is a way to describe these four laws together in a simple formula. In a given moment, the S-curve tells us how happy we will be when we experience some level of a reality and hold certain expectations. To predict happiness for a future time, we need to draw the S-curve taking into account possible shifts in the level of expectations. The curve shifts to the right if expectations increase and to the left if expectations decrease.

OPTIMIZING HAPPINESS

It is now the moment to play with our simple model of human psychology. The two basic ingredients of our potion are reality and expectations.

Reality is the car you own, the activities you do, or the neighborhood you live in.

In order to create an operational model of happiness, we will need to make some specific assumptions about how expectations move. Remember that expectations are a function of the past and of the others. To make things simple, we will focus on the role of the past on setting expectations. For example, we propose a simple law of motion of expectations. We will say that expectations change on a daily basis. Expectations for the next day, *New Expectation*, are equal to today's expectations, but nudged up or down a bit depending on today's difference between reality and expectations. If today's reality is better than expectations, then the new expectation will be higher than today's expectation. We use the following adaptation equation, proposed by the marketing professor Luc Wathieu, in which the shift in expectations is proportional to the gains and losses:[2]

SHIFT IN EXPECTATIONS *equals*
Speed of Adaptation × (REALITY *minus* EXPECTATION)

The *speed of adaptation* is a number between zero and one that regulates how fast the expectations change. The speed of adaptation can change depending on the category of good, or type of activity. A speed of adaptation equal to one implies that expectations immediately adapt to the current reality. A speed of adaptation equal to zero means that expectations or references never change. A lower speed of adaptation, say of 10 percent, means that it takes at least ten days to adapt to a new reality.

We now have a simple model of human psychology that may seem basic, but at least it is fundamental and complete. That is, the model contains sufficient elements to produce predictions on how much happiness will be experienced under different scenarios of reality, which means that we now have a formula for happiness!

It may not be the perfect formula, but it operates on a set of laws and it offers a concrete starting point—which is what we like to work with.

For example, the formula for calculating new expectations we gave earlier does not take into account social comparison. But for now the simpler formula is good enough. Let's put our laws of happiness to the test.

A GROUP OF FRIENDS MEETS A GENIE

Three very close friends decided it was time to pack their bags and hit the road for a vacation! The destination picked was the ancient Mayan ruins in Chichen Itza, Mexico, where they would spend their time in contact with nature, hiking the mountains, and studying the ruins of this ancient civilization. On one sunny afternoon during the trip, one of them tripped on something half buried in the ground. "Ouch!"—You could hear Frank shouting so loudly that his voice echoed far beyond the mountains. "What is this in the middle of the trail?" Mariah, who was right behind him, kneeled quickly and rose back up with a strange-looking object in her hands: "A golden shiny bottle," she said as Jack approached.

As they watched her examine it, a curious smoke started blowing out of the bottle and, with a loud pop, a genie in the form of a Mayan woman appeared out of midair. With their mouths agape, they watched the figure perform rituals as she told them they would have the amazing opportunity to spend one hundred rare coins in exactly fifty days, stipulating that "You can spend the coins only within this dream life and in one, and only one, category of consumption, whether it is cars, boats, traveling, parties, or anything else."

Since our friends had to commute to work using slow public transportation, they decided to have a contest to see who gets the most happiness in spending their windfall of one hundred coins on a better mode of commuting for the next fifty days. The cars they had available for rentals were an economy car, a midsize car, a full-size car, and a luxury sports car. For a day of rental, an economy car costs one coin, a midsize costs two coins, a full-size costs three coins, and a luxury car costs four coins. They could also take the bus, which was free. Since our friends have a total of one hundred coins each, they must use these coins wisely to rent the right type of car for the right duration. Before you read further, think for a moment what you would do in this situation. Would you spend the hundred coins to rent a luxury sports car for twenty-five days, and then take the bus for the remaining twenty-five days? Or would you rather spend the hundred coins to rent a midsize car for the entire fifty days? Let us see what each of our characters has planned.

Our focus in this example is to understand the mechanism of adaptation. Hence, we ignore the effects of social comparison.

Nouveau Riche Jack

Jack feels as if he has just won the lottery: He is impatient and decides to make reality very exciting for the first twenty-five days by leasing a fancy Porsche. Of course, the Porsche costs four coins per day, and in day twenty-five Jack runs out of coins, returns his Porsche to the dealer, and takes the bus for the remaining twenty-five days. What is the recording that this decision will produce in his happiness seismogram? How many happydons in total does he get?[3]

At the beginning, Jack is extremely happy, enjoying the performance of the car and the status accorded to him while driving it. Since his expectation has not yet adapted, he finds a great deal of excitement and novelty speeding on the highways while listening to loud music. The very first day he gets 8 happydons. This excitement and enjoyment fades away little by little as he becomes used to it, and as the expectations adapt, the gap between reality and expectations closes. The happydons derived from the Porsche decrease to 7, 5, 4, 3, and 2 as days pass. As day twenty-five approaches, his enjoyment has greatly diminished—what used to be exciting and joyful is no longer the same way now. Still, he managed to enjoy a total of 110 happydons during the first 25 days from driving the Porsche.

When the car gets returned to the dealer, Jack experiences a great deal of unhappiness, a sort of negative blow that exceeds greatly in intensity the positive moments of the past. He gets negative 16 happydons the very first day that he travels on a bus. At this moment Jack predicts that he will stay this unhappy for the remaining twenty-five days, but fortunately this is not correct. Expectations will also adapt downward, closing the gap between reality and expectations. Unhappiness will be lasting, but the intensity will diminish and, approaching day fifty Jack will be doing okay, losing only 4 happydons per day.

How much happiness has Jack bought with this budget? The happiness seismogram, or happiness in each day, is calculated using the reality minus the expectation in each day.[4] The total happiness is then the area between the curve and the zero line. In Jack's case, the area between the happiness recording and the zero line is positive during the first twenty-five days by 110 happydons, but in the next twenty-five days he loses 215 happydons, and the total is negative 105. Negative! How is that possible if he won one hundred coins to be spent on anything? How come his happiness is not positive or at least zero? Well, loss aversion explains it. Jack's unhappiness after losing the car far outweighs the pleasure he had while owning it. He's like one of those teenagers who spend their entire monthly budget in the first week and then sit at home frustrated for the other three weeks of the month.

Stable Frank

Our next character is Frank, the one who tripped on the bottle. Frank finds Jack's plan to be a naïve and immature and he thinks he can do better. Although Frank adores cars as much as Jack, he tries to control his initial excitement and think in terms of the long run. He chooses to lease a less fancy car at a lower cost so that he is able to enjoy it for a longer period of time. That is, he simply divides the budget of one hundred coins by fifty, the number of periods, and sets his expense at this level. So Frank leases a midsize car that costs two coins per day. It is indeed half as fancy as Jack's.

Frank's solution is quite clever in a world with zero speed of adaptation. If the only law that matters is that of diminishing sensitivity, and the first sip tastes better than the second, which in turn tastes better than the third, the optimal solution is to spread out consumption evenly across time. That is, take one sip every day.

Because the speed of adaptation is 10 percent, not 0 percent, Frank experiences less happiness as time passes. He is quite excited at the beginning, getting six happydons per day. Of course, this is less than the eight happydons that Jack got from the Porsche. Because of adaptation, expectations increase over time, and Frank's happiness gets smaller as days pass. At the end of the fifty days he is almost fully adapted, getting less than one happydon per day. There is one major difference between Jack and Frank: Frank will never experience negative emotions. Frank may not have driven a Porsche, but at least he avoids the embarrassment of having to catch the bus after driving a Porsche!

In fact, Frank does much better than Jack, as he derives a total happiness of positive 110 happydons. Compared to the negative 105 of Jack, the calculation shows how powerful loss aversion is.

Most of us hate to sacrifice any standard of living to which we've become accustomed. As creatures of habit, we will actually figure out ways to maintain living standards and habits. For instance, wealthy people who start losing their money sometimes choose to remain in their big mansions with a much lower daily budget rather than move to a smaller house and have more money on hand. In contrast, an average person who never had lived in a mansion can enjoy living in a small home with a modest income.

That Frank does much better than Jack shows that if people strive to be happy, they will resist losing. And this means that people will either maintain or increase those activities and consumption goods that they have been consuming for a long time. Habit persistence is a logical consequence of the laws of happiness! Indeed, for goods consumed over a long period, a reduction from their habitual levels will produce a loss. For example, if you are used to having a cleaner for your apartment once a week and you need to cut this cost and start cleaning the place yourself, the loss will be great and will make you unhappy. If you had always done the service yourself, it is not that big a burden because, well, it's a habit. In fact, the best predictor of future behavior is past behavior, and the best predictor of future consumption is past consumption.

Lottery winners, Hollywood stars, and sports heroes that have made large amounts of money and spent them on luxury goods often ask themselves this question: How come having so much has not bought me happiness? Simply put, adaptation washed it away. And while this adaptation takes place in our subconscious, we can outsmart it by anticipating adaptation and not letting it sneak up on us. Let us see how.

Prudent Mariah

Our job as engineers is to set the *happiness problem* as a well-formulated optimization problem. And what is a well-formulated optimization problem? Well, a well-formulated optimization problem consists of three elements. The first element is *decision variables*—in this case, we have fifty decision variables, which is what we need to specify how much to spend in each of the fifty days. The second element is the constraints on these decision variables. The main constraint is that the total expense needs to meet the budget. Thus, the sum of the fifty decision variables is supposed to be equal to one hundred. The second constraint is that the decision variables need to be positive integers (0, 1, 2, and so on . . .).

The third element is the objective function—the function we wish to maximize. The objective function is based on calculating reality and expectations period after periods. Reality is given by our decision on how much to spend. The second law dictates that expectations adapt. One possible way in which this adjustment may happen is to calculate expectations in the next period as a weighted average of the current expectations and the current consumption. Once we have reality minus expectations period by period, we then use the S-curve to calculate the happiness in the period. Doing this for all fifty periods produces the happiness seismogram. The sum of the happiness obtained in all the periods gives the total happiness, which is our objective function.

Observe how the objective function depends on the decision variables. The question is: what arrangement of the decision variables is feasible and also yields the highest value for the objective function?

Computers are great at dealing with well-formulated optimization problems. If the problem is not too complex, then the computer will try many combinations and return the best arrangement of the decision variables that yield the highest possible value of the objective function. The computer will take care that such an arrangement is feasible, that is, it satisfies all the constraints. If the problem is too large or too complex, then the computer will produce something close to the optimal solution.

So, the group of friends is still out there trying to figure out who will get the most out of the genie-in-the-bottle experience. Mariah, who dug the bottle out of the ground, knows computers. When faced with this situation of the hundred coins and how to best spend them, she quickly got her PDA out of her pocket, entered the happiness problem in a spreadsheet, and used the solver tool to find the optimal way to spend the coins. Her PDA computer returned the seismogram representing the maximum happiness possible using these hundred coins.

Mariah's solution involves a lot of restraint and patience, and she doesn't know yet whether she will have sufficient courage, willpower, and conviction to implement the solution. According to her own results, she is supposed to take the bus for the first two days, and then lease an affordable car for one coin per day. The optimal program requires that she hold on to this car for many days. A bit before the twenty-fifth day, she can then trade up for a better model. Why wait so long? Because otherwise, she would increase expectations too soon and early increases are expensive! Early increases in expectations subtract happiness from the remaining days. It is cheaper to delay the increases, so that expectations increase later. Indeed, Mariah can then enjoy two further increases, which includes using the Porsche during the last eight days. Mariah attains the maximum happiness possible within the boundaries of our model, which is +145 happydons. Mariah was not richer, nor was she genetically more inclined to experience happiness. The laws of happiness apply to her the same way they do to Jack and Frank. Mariah was simply smarter, as she understood how happiness worked. She was able to engineer a happier experience!

Mariah's optimal solution strikes the right balance between spreading out consumption and creating an increasing sequence. Spreading out consumption counteracts diminishing sensitivity, and an increasing pattern counteracts adaptation.

Mariah, smarter than the guys, concluded: "Jack was impatient. He had the greatest enjoyment initially, but could not sustain consumption above his reference levels, and could not avoid feeling the loss of cutting back. Frank understood this, and did the simplest thing to avoid losses: He settled for consumption that never decreases. But, his initial purchase was costly and the adaptation he experienced from the very beginning limited his overall happiness. After this analysis, Mariah figured out her solution to this challenge, and also the secret of happiness is to use a *crescendo* strategy, always going from less to more. To make this feasible, it is important to keep low levels of consumption at the beginning and, even better, find the right time in life to initiate new habits. Mariah understood the logic of crescendo.

Suppose you want to maintain constant happiness. To do so, you need to follow the advice of Confucius: "The one who would be in constant happiness must frequently change." Do as Mariah: maintain an increasing consumption plan, making sure that there is always a gap between reality and expectations.

One way to put these ideas into practice is to stagger the acquisition of better and better possessions, rather than jumping right to the best. We have a friend at the Central Bank of Guatemala who did exactly that when deciding on which new motorcycle to buy:

> I currently own a Honda Twister 250. I'm happy with my current bike, but I would like to buy a new one with a more powerful engine. There are two candidates: the Triumph Bonneville and the BMW R1150R.
>
> Technologically, the BMW motorcycle is superior, because it's got a transmission axle, instead of a chain (which requires less maintenance); it's

also got ABS brakes and a better suspension system. In general it is a bigger bike, both in physical size and engine, and also a more expensive one. If I had to buy only one motorcycle for the rest of my life, I would purchase the BMW.

On the other hand, the Triumph has a "retro" kind of style which is very charming, and I like the fact that it is lower; therefore, I believe that I am still in a phase of my life in which I need a motorcycle that is less intimidating, besides being cheaper.

Then the reasoning goes like this: buy the Triumph now and enjoy all its advantages and properties. Eventually, in an indeterminate future, buy the BMW R1150R (or a similar model). Though this implies not having the best possible motorcycle since the beginning, it allows me to follow an increasing path on the quality of the motorcycles. According to this theory of shifting expectations, it would also have the additional advantage of being compatible with a sustainable path of happiness, since happiness, as I understand, is more a function of attaining successive improvements in consumption than of attaining certain absolute levels of consumption.

Yes! This strategy is exactly the right way to go! Maybe you can also think about an example like this in your life, when you consciously analyzed your consumption decisions to maximize your happiness.

Saving the Best for Last

Remember, Jack leased a Porsche at four coins per day for *the first* twenty-five days. When he got the car right away, his end result was a happiness loss of 105. If he had leased the Porsche for the *last* twenty-five days, he would have achieved a happiness gain of +115. Hence, saving the best for last is a simple way to get assured happiness, because it uses the crescendo strategy.

A group of friends went for vacation to Croatia. Croatia has two important national parks, Krka and Plitvice. For many, Plitvice is more spectacular than Krka. This group visited Krka first, and had a very enjoyable day—it has some nice waterfalls and a unique monastery located in a small river island. Three days later, they visited Plitvice and were startled by the beauty of the cascades and lakes. All in all, they left with nice memories of the two days spent visiting parks. Later in their trip they met a couple that had visited Plitvice first and had just returned from visiting Krka. This couple felt that, compared to Plitvice, Krka was not nearly as beautiful. In fact, they even seemed to be disappointed with the day spent at Krka. They were right, Krka might not be worth visiting only a few days after Plitvice, but it is definitely worth visiting before Plitvice.

Therefore, it's not the inherent value of something that matters most, but how that value compares with what immediately preceded it.

The same resources, but with different sequencing and ordering, produce different levels of happiness.

Most executives will acknowledge that one key to successful management is managing expectations to motivate maximum productivity. Basically, there are two possible ways to do this. The first is to overpromise and later underdeliver, and the second is to underpromise and later overdeliver. If we have convinced you that happiness is associated with creating increasing sequences, you'll probably agree that underpromising and overdelivering is the right way to go.

Promises of promotions, bonuses, vacation days, and reductions in workload are easy to make. And they may temporarily get workers to go the extra mile. But if these promises are not fulfilled, then employees will quickly become demoralized. To build credibility, it is better to underpromise and later overdeliver.

In one company, there were three division executives contending for the general director's position. One of them presented an ambitious expansion plan for the company. The proposal was so impressive and ambitious that the board decided to appoint this division executive to the position. However, his proposed plan quickly turned out to be infeasible and a year later this executive was fired from the company.

COPING WITH LOSSES

Suppose you are Jack in day twelve. By now, you have spent half of your budget, and you have fifty-some coins, your budget for the remaining thirty-eight days. Suddenly, you realize that cannot sustain the current expense of four coins a day you are used to. Should you continue with the initial plan of spending four coins per day until day twenty-five, return the car, and end up with unhappiness of −105? Clearly there must be a better strategy!

Let's enter into the computer the following problem. Maximize the total happiness during the time that remains, thirty-eight days, given the budget that remains, fifty-two coins, and considering that our current expectations, rather than equal to zero, are closer to our current consumption level of four.

The solution that the computer gives to this problem is as follows. The best would be for him to return the Porsche immediately and then use the bus for some days. In this way, Jack will experience a large loss, but his expectations will adjust day after day to the new situation. Moreover, based on the law of diminishing sensitivity, this initial unhappiness will be somehow cushioned. Once his expectation falls sufficiently, he could imitate Mariah and go gradually from an economy car back to a Porsche.[5]

If the times call for tightening the belt, the optimal strategy is to begin with a painful initial phase, in which the goal is to lower expectations as fast as possible. In due time, we will adapt to the new circumstances. One thing is for sure: it will take time.

Hardships lower expectations and create new comparisons, enabling us to see the world in more absolute terms and with a much wider perspective. In his book *Happiness, Pleasure, and Judgment,* Allen Parducci, a psychology professor at UCLA, argues that past peaks of unhappiness increase future happiness.[6]

INSIDE THE BLACK BOX

Suppose that instead of one hundred coins and fifty days, we have just three coins and three days. In the first day, you can spend zero, one, two, or three coins. If we spend zero on day one, then there are many possibilities open for days two and three. If we spend three coins on the first day, then there is nothing left for the second and third days. If we spend two coins on the first day, then we have two remaining possibilities: spend the last coin in the second period or in the third. This logic gives us a total of ten possibilities.

Take one of these ten possible sequences. Knowing the consumption on each day and how the adaptation rate moves, we can compare reality minus expectations in each day. This allows us to calculate the happiness each day and the total happiness associated with each possibility.

What do we learn? Not surprisingly, the three plans that score the highest in terms of happiness are those having the less-to-more property: consumption never decreases. In this case, the optimal sequence is (o, 1, 2), the second best is (o, o, 3), and the third best is (1, 1, 1). In contrast, consuming all resources at the beginning, (3, o, o), produces the most unhappy sequence.

For sufficiently small problems, computers can enumerate all possibilities. For larger problems, computers use "implicit enumeration techniques" to find the optimum combination among millions. This is what Mariah, the wisest of the three friends used to find the optimal way of spending her hundred coins over fifty days.

For even larger problems, computers can find near-optimal solutions that, although not optimal for sure, definitely beat our intuition by taking personal subjectivity out of the equation. Of course, all this assumes a well-defined problem: decision variables, constraints, and objective function.

THE "REVERSE" BRAVE NEW WORLD

Aldous Huxley's *Brave New World* describes a reality where human beings live in a technology-addicted reality with no violence, where everything is carefully programmed For example, babies are born in laboratories, people take daily drugs to avoid depression, and movies with sensory stimulation are the most popular entertainment.[7] Within this controlled society, a man senses that his relationship with a young woman won't be able to develop beyond what is allowed within the society and, therefore, starts questioning the entire system. The author questions many of the things that we take for granted nowadays. The message is that social happiness cannot be engineered through technology and control.

What we propose is a "reverse brave new world." In this world, the idea is not to inherit the peak level of technology. Rather, the idea is to experiment on numerous incremental technological improvements. To do so, the key is to start with an extremely low level. In this imaginary world, to maximize people's happiness children are born in medieval-type societies: no democracy, no electricity, no PlayStation, no television, no Internet, no MP3 player.

We would provide the children with basic goods such as food, shelter, and medical care from the beginning. When they are age five, electricity would be introduced, providing them with great joy and excitement. Little by little, appliances that can be used with electricity such as toys that run with batteries or escalators would appear in their lives. Each one of them will give them great joy. When the children are age ten, the television would appear—black and white, of course. Three year later, the color TV will be discovered. This pattern would continue until they are middle-aged, when computers, mobile phones, and the Internet would be introduced.

Of course, this is an imaginary and unreal possibility. Still, the message is clear: To maximize happiness, not everything has to be made available right away. Little children will be just fine if they do not get used to having the best of everything. The optimal approach is that of beginning low, setting a low reference, and then moving up incrementally. If you have never seen or had some good, then you don't miss it. As one of our colleagues said: it is better to postpone as much as possible bringing your kids to an expensive amusement park. Once you go, your kids will want to return every year!

You can easily apply this approach whenever you take up a new sport or hobby. Rather than going out and buying the best equipment available, we would recommend that you start out with modest, used equipment and then upgrade gradually. Of course, this approach also helps you limit your expenses if you quit the sport or hobby after the first few lessons.

There is no doubt that technology has offered our generation a sequence of improvements. According to our model, computers and mobile phones have increased the happiness of many, by providing an increasing set of advantages. No matter how incredible a technology is, its contribution to happiness depends as much on the improvement per se as on the incremental rate at which the technology is administered. Let's take petroleum-powered technologies such as cars and planes, for example. These technologies are mature, in the sense that we are quite used to them, and we do not expect major breakthroughs in their efficiency. Thus, the happiness potential of these technologies is rather limited. Of course, as a society we are trapped, and we really cannot live without them.

Still, if we were able to take an absolute perspective, oil is one of the most incredible blessings, giving us a cheap and malleable source of energy that has transformed our society and has liberated the human condition in many ways. But now, as we experience the drawbacks of contamination and crowded roads, we are growing increasingly unhappy about this blessing. Commuting is, in fact, a big source of unhappiness. But to take the absolute perspective is not difficult: just try walking to work one day (it might take eight hours!), and you will start to appreciate commuting.

It would have been much better for us if the petroleum-powered technologies had become available in smaller increments, giving us hope for a better future. In contrast, electronic technology still has many improvements in store, and hence it has the ability to keep our faith in progress. Of course, once this technology levels off, the excitement will also wane. Hopefully, through our research efforts and inventiveness, new technologies may emerge in the future. Or, better yet, someday we will learn to be happier with what we have by training our brains to take an absolute, rather than relative, perspective.

Here is another application of the crescendo idea. When couples move to a new house, they often wonder what's best: to decorate the house all at once, perhaps by getting a larger mortgage loan, or to live with modest furniture and then make improvements in the house little by little, as the couple's economic condition improves. Our model has a clear recommendation: always go from less to more. Yes, by having the apartment totally ready, one would definitely have a big jump in happiness, as Jack did, but Mariah got more happiness from planning an increasing sequence. Leaving room for future improvement not only saves interest payments, it also creates opportunities for us to reach small milestones, and this in turn increases total happiness, which is our ultimate goal!

In summary, our model supports commonsense advice of frugality. It is better to postpone expensive consumption if there is a limited budget. Make sure you choose the right ordering of events, always trying to ensure an increasing path! The crescendo (less to more) philosophy also generates happiness from anticipation. Looking into the future, Mariah can only be optimistic.

HAPPINESS IN ACTION

The next time you plan a trip, think strategically about how you order your itinerary. Rather than visiting the most spectacular museum, beach, or temple first, save those experiences for the end of your trip. Try to order your schedule from least to most spectacular or exciting. Do the same with the choice of hotels. That way, you'll enjoy the lesser sites in the earlier part of your trip, and build up to the really memorable experiences.

CHAPTER 7

The Fifth Law of Happiness

Satiation

I went to see high mountains, I went to see oceans. Only I had not seen at my very doorstep, the dew drop glistening on the ear of the corn.   —Rabindranath Tagore

The four laws that we have introduced are very useful to understand the formation of habits and the incremental strategies required to maximize happiness. But we are still missing one essential element to understand that there is more to life than just habits. This element, the spice of life, is variety. Variety, as we will argue, will be a consequence of the fifth law of happiness.

Suppose you just got back from a weeklong holiday in the Bahamas, where you spent the days relaxing on a beautiful beach sipping colorful cocktails. When the vacation ends, you return home and dive back into your daily routine. The following Friday afternoon a friend calls saying she just found a great deal online for a last-minute weekend package in St. Bart's: "You won't believe it," she shouts excitedly. "We can have nice drinks by the pool every day!" It sounds like a great trip, but you're hardly motivated to go since you just got back from the Bahamas the previous weekend. You'll probably be very interested after a few months of miserable winter weather or after a rough period at work, but not now. Why is that? It is because you are satiated with a beach vacation.

> *The Fifth Law—Satiation: Recent consumption reduces the happiness intensity of subsequent consumption; and recent abstinence increases the happiness of subsequent consumption.*

It doesn't take a marine biologist to know that a sea lion that has just eaten twenty pounds of herring is a happy sea lion. After the meal, she lounges in the sunshine as the waves crash on the rocks, her happiness seismogram reaching a daily peak of $+10$ happydons. Recall that the happiness seismogram is the hypothetical recording of moment happiness over time. Total happiness, measured in happydons, is the area between the seismogram and the zero line. But let's ask a simple question: Would twenty pounds of herring always give the sea lion 10 happydons? If she had just eaten a few hours earlier, she probably wouldn't enjoy the additional twenty pounds of fish all that much (after all, even sea lions, with all that blubber, can still feel stuffed). But if she has not eaten for two days, then she will be very hungry, and the twenty pounds of herrings today will be warmly welcome and may even give her more than 10 happydons.

Along with food and vacations, there are many other experiences the enjoyment of which depends on the time elapsed since you last had that experience. This happens because the consumption of goods or experiences creates a memory that diminishes over time, which acts in the same way as the satiation level for food.

Unless you are a huge fan of some actor or actress, would you want to watch a movie that you saw just last week? After some time has passed, the images from the movie or the vacation memories will fade, and once again you will be able to fully enjoy that same experience almost as if it were the first time.

When we think about how much pleasure we derive from a particular food, it is necessary to take into account how full we are, or our "satiation level." The satiation level can be positive when we are full, zero when we are neutral, even negative if we are hungry. Satiation levels depend, of course, on the quantity we recently consumed. The passage of time lowers these satiation levels. Satiation levels also depend on the adaptation levels. A person who is not accustomed to spicy food will reach his limit quickly. Others who have adapted to it can eat lots of spicy foods at every meal.

It is an unavoidable neurological fact that any kind of pleasure has a limit that makes lasting happiness impossible. The more frequently a signal is sent to the brain, the less able the brain is to process it as new information, which lowers our potential for satisfaction. This is due to the so-called refractory period, during which a single cell is not able to fire the same signal again for a while. It is the same when you scratch an itch. Scratching overloads the nerves near the itch and causes them to react less to the itch, but after a few seconds the itch returns worse than ever and you will need to scratch even more to receive the same relief as before.

Even if you were the richest man on Earth, your happiness would diminish because of satiation with having too much. To understand that unlimited money cannot give unlimited amounts of pleasure, and that variety and novelty can indeed increase happiness, it is essential to account for satiation.

Satiation is closely related to the Law of Diminishing Sensitivity. Basically, if we've enjoyed something recently we become satiated and having more doesn't bring as much enjoyment. But, if it has been a while we will develop a craving and enjoy great pleasure when that craving is satisfied. Thus, if satiation is low (for example, you have not eaten at all during the day), then the same consumption (dinner) will provide greater enjoyment as compared to when satiation is high (you just had a big, late lunch).

How does satiation fits into our framework? Recall our fundamental equation of happiness.

HAPPINESS is an S-curve of
REALITY *minus* SHIFTING EXPECTATIONS
adjusted for SATIATION

Let us see exactly how to adjust the happiness S-curve to account for satiation. We will see that the happiness obtained in a given period of time depends on both the expectation level and the satiation level. Let's use a simple example.

How much would you enjoy one slice of pizza? "It depends," you say. On what? "Well, the enjoyment is greater if I am hungry," you reply.

After eating your first slice of your favorite pizza—which, let's say, gives you +5 happydons—you're still hungry, so you have a second slice. How much enjoyment do you expect to obtain from this second slice? Most likely, the total satisfaction from the second slice will be less, say +2 happydons, because of the Law of Diminishing Sensitivity.

So, one slice of pizza can give you +5 happydons if you are hungry and can give you +2 happydons if you have just eaten a slice. The reason is that the satiation level, which we call S, starts out at $S = 0$ before you eat any pizza, but jumps up to $S = 1$ as soon as you have eaten the first piece. Satiation level increases with consumption and reverts to zero over time without consumption.

How much enjoyment you would obtain from one slice of pizza at 6 p.m., if you had already had one slice of pizza at noon?

Let's suppose that the satiation level at 6 p.m. is equal to $S = 0.5$. The way to calculate happiness from the S-curve is to start from the satiation level. The incremental happiness from S to S *plus one slice of pizza* gives the satisfaction of this particular slice of pizza. In this case, the incremental happiness form 0.5 to 1.5 gives +3 happydons. When $S = 0$, the incremental happiness from 0 to 1 gives +5 happydons; and when $S = 1$, the incremental happiness from 1 to 2 slices gives +2 happydons. Therefore, we can now calculate the happydons that one slice of pizza produces for any satiation level.

Hence, each instance of consumption yields happiness, but reduces hunger. *Later consumption provides enjoyment starting from this baseline satiation level.* The speed at which satiation levels decay during periods of no consumption is called the *speed of satiation.*[1]

Our laws predict that basic goods will produce more satiation than adaptive goods. For adaptive goods, expectations increase with consumption. As expectations increase, there is less buildup of satiation with future consumption. The reason is that the buildup of satiation is a function of consumption in excess of expectations. If consumption is high but expectations are equally high, then there is little satiation. In contrast, for nonadaptive or basic goods, expectations move slowly. Hence, satiation builds up based on absolute level of consumption.

Hence, we could say that *adaptation mitigates satiation*—once a habit is formed, a consumer is able to sustain large intakes without experiencing satiation. Everyone enjoys music, but the taste for a style of music develops over time. For instance, somebody used to classical music may listen to it for the entire day without experiencing satiation. However, if a person not used to classical music buys an MP3 player and listens to these symphonies, he may be easily satiated after five minutes of listening. Later on, once this person has made a habit of listening to classical music, he might be able to enjoy symphonies for much of the day.

It is very much as Adam Smith observed in *The Wealth of Nations:* "The desire of food is limited in every man by the narrow capacity of the human stomach, but the desire of the conveniences and ornaments of buildings, dress, equipage, and household furniture, seems to have no limit or certain boundary."[2]

THE CURSE OF OVERCONSUMPTION

The story "The Midas Plague" depicts a world where robots overproduce far beyond what is needed for the society.[3] In such a society, poor people are forced to consume frantically. Poor folks live in sprawling mansions with quarter-acre ballrooms. And yet, the poor are unhappy because there is almost too much consumption to keep up with. In contrast, the rich live austerely in small houses, with smaller cars and simpler gadgets. Upper-class people are allowed to work, and actually are happier because they get a relief from the constant consumption that plagues the poor.

In our own research, we have shown mathematically that indeed the counterintuitive outcome of lower happiness could occur when consumption increases.[4] Too much consumption saturates our senses, and pleasure declines.

In one study, lottery winners actually reported that they experienced significantly less pleasure from mundane daily activities than they previously had.[5]

Suppose you are offered a prize of six bottles of wine or six museum passes, which you can use over time. Common sense would suggest that you should spread out the consumption over time. Again, mathematically we can determine the optimal duration over which to spread out the consumption. For a product or experience that is highly satiating you should spread out the consumption over a longer period than for a good that has low satiation. You may enjoy six bottles of wine over the next six weeks, but you may visit a museum only once every four months, and thus take almost two years to experience it six times. When it comes to partying, eating out, and taking trips, it is wise to slow down a bit and not let satiation dull your joy.

EXPLORATION AND EXPLOITATION

In Samuel Johnson's novel *Rasselas*,[6] the prince of Abyssinia lives in a "happy valley" with all worldly comforts provided. Yet he finds himself bored and plots his escape to experience life in the outside world. His philosopher companion asks, "Look round and tell me which of your wants is without supply: if you want nothing, how are you unhappy?" The Prince replies, "When I see the kids and the lambs chasing one another, I fancy that I should be happy if I had something to pursue. But, possessing all that I can want, I find one day and one hour exactly like another, except that the latter is still more tedious than the former. . . . I have already enjoyed too much; give me something to desire."

Is satiation a blessing or a curse? If you have recently consumed beyond your adaptation level—too much popcorn at the movies—you experience satiation. Satiation naturally promotes an interest in novelty and variety, and you may think, "I'll enjoy some Coca Cola while my satiation level for the popcorn decreases."

Adaptation and satiation present a conflict. Adaptation produces the effect of the more you get, the more you want. This logic induces either complete abstinence ("going cold turkey") or increasing consumption rates (continued indulgence). By contrast, satiation produces the opposite marginal effect: the more you get, the less you want, which leads to a desire to seek variety. If our laws of happiness are correct, we should feel the tension between these two forces in determining the optimal allocation of consumption.

What happens over time when we can choose between competing activities? What is the optimal approach? To make things simple, let's consider two activities: tennis and golf. Every week, we need to decide which of the two is best. If the speed of satiation and the speed of adaptation are the same for both activities, then the optimal plan is to alternate between the two activities.

What if one of the two activities, say golf, has a higher speed of adaptation? The optimal plan is as follows. During the first weeks, one is better off rotating between tennis and golf: T, G, T, G, ... As weeks pass, and one adapts to golf faster than to tennis, it is best to start leaning toward golf: G, G, T, G, G, T, G, . . . Eventually, the optimal thing to do is to abandon tennis and permanently switch to golf: T, G, G, G, G. . . .

The optimal pattern follows the scheme of exploration and exploitation. Due to the variety-seeking behavior induced by satiation, you should start off switching back and forth between tennis and golf. That is, we begin with a phase of exploration with lots of variety. As the adaptation level for golf increases beyond that for tennis, you will likely choose tennis less frequently as time passes, to avoid the withdrawal from golf. At some point, you may decide to permanently switch to golf.

This is the phase of exploitation, where we stay with the things that we like the most. In fact, casual observation indicates that young people seek variety in their activities, whereas older people tend to settle on a few, very established habits. Don't you remember your grandpa always reading the paper, playing chess, or bowling?

> *Low adaptation levels make variety and novelty optimal. High adaptation levels make variety and novelty suboptimal, as we do better by sticking to our habits.*

As a child, Rafael was one of those kids who had a schedule almost as busy as a grownup businessman's. He went from school to judo classes twice a week, swimming lessons three times a week, and computer lessons every day—not to mention the clubs he participated in at school, such as cycling and soccer. During his teenage years, he tried hiking, climbing, and horseracing. Then, at the age of twenty-eight, he discovered his real passion: diving. Fifteen years later, diving remained Rafael's passion, taking him to oceans all over the world exploring marine life and shipwrecks.

Thus, the highly criticized explosion of extracurricular activities for young kids may turn out to be a great idea after all. Trying different activities in one's younger years not only expands one's horizons; it also provides the contrast in happiness derived from adaptation and satiation from each activity. Then later in life we can stay with the few activities that consistently give us the most pleasure.

VARIETY AND CRESCENDO

In the previous chapter, we concentrated on a single adaptive good and gave the recipe that the optimal allocation of budget was to ensure an increasing sequence. But what is the optimal budget allocation when facing multiple goods?

Often, we have the possibility of choosing both the activity (for example, cycling, golf, or tennis; or type of restaurant) as well as the quality or budget for the activity (for example, buy more expensive sports gear, play on better golf courses, or go to more expensive restaurants). With all of these factors in play, how is one supposed to optimize happiness?

When we enter this complex problem into a computer and run our optimization, the solution we obtain is the following.[7] Consumption alternates between different goods and activities, and the budget allocated to these increases over time. An example of such a pattern would be an individual who alternates among forms of entertainment (restaurants, plays, and concerts) and, over time, as he gets used to its aesthetic pleasures, increases his budget for entertainment (more expensive restaurants, plays, and concerts).

LIFE SIMPLICITY

We have seen two smart ways to handle adaptation and satiation. The first is the strategy of exploration and exploitation, where we first try multiple activities and then settle on a few of them. The second is to combine variety with crescendo. On the activities that we choose to engage, make sure you plan for an increasing budget over time. There is a third question that we would like to address: how many habits to initiate?

To answer this question, we run our fundamental equation using the following example. You can choose among three evening activities: go to the gym, go to the cinema, and take dancing lessons. Should you go to the gym every time, or rotate among the three activities?

Assume that the three activities are similar, in the sense that they have the same speed of satiation and the same speed of adaptation. We will fix the common speed of satiation, and vary the common speed of adaptation. Our laws produce three patterns for the optimal sequence:

- If the common speed of adaptation is low, then the optimal plan is to alternate among the *three* activities, and hence counteract the effect of satiation.

- If the common speed of adaptation is moderate, then the optimal plan is to alternate between *two* of the three activities and to disregard the third activity entirely.
- If the common speed of adaptation is high, then the optimal plan is to choose just *one* of the activities and stay with it.

For goods and activities with a low speed of adaptation, variety mitigates the effects of satiation. As the speed of adaptation increases, then we still want to alternate between activities, but it is better to reduce the total number of these activities. In the extreme for sufficiently high speed of adaptation, one may not want to alternate and would prefer to stay just with one type of activity. For this reason, given a choice between goods with multiple speeds of adaptation, it is better to avoid the consumption of those that are highly adaptive as they will drag us into obsessive behaviors.

Our point is the following. There are a myriad of activities and habits we can engage in. Even if you were to have all the time, money, and motivation you could ask for, what maximizes happiness is neither to engage in all of them nor to have too restrictive a set of activities. Rather, the optimal pattern is to alternate among a few selected habits and happily abstain from all the others. This holds true for evening activities and sports as well as for other choices such as which type of food we try, or which friends to spend time with.

Do you know the story of Sona and the vina (a kind of violin), taught in Buddhist philosophy? The Buddha asked Sona, an accomplished musician who was seeking spiritual guidance, to make music with a vina whose strings he had loosened. Sona laughed and told the Buddha that he could not produce music, as the strings were too loose. Buddha then proceeded to wind the strings very tight. Of course, what came out were high-pitched squeaks. Sona then took the vina from the Buddha's hands and tuned it just right to make beautiful music. By this example Buddha taught Sona that the middle path lying between too much and too little is the way to enlightenment. In Western culture, Aristotle elaborated the concept of the golden mean under the maxim *in medio virtus:* there is virtue in moderation.

Total happiness may, therefore, be maximized by deliberately choosing only a few habituating goods. May be that is why some parents try to keep children from acquiring time-consuming or expensive habits. The anthropologist Rentato Rosaldo argues that repetition brings about the ordinary and the normal, which in turn makes people comfortable and happy.[8]

Our law of satiation gives an extra twist to the commonsense idea that, yes, variety and novelty help. But in combination with the rule of adaptation, we show that moderation in the total number of habits is optimal. Believe it or not, we have proven this assertion mathematically, in what we call the life simplicity theorem. Our laws also recommend that over time, one is happier if one focuses on a few well-established habits. To put it in a humorous way, at a certain age it is OK to react as Henny Youngman did: "When I read about the dangers of drinking, I gave up reading."

CRAVING

What we call happiness comes from the satisfaction of needs
which have been dammed up to a high degree.
 —Sigmund Freud, *Civilization and Its Discontents*

The *San Diego Union-Tribune* carried the following piece on May 12, 2008: "To Help Nonprofit Group, Woman Eats on a Dollar a Day." The article reads: "As she concluded her quest to eat for 30 days on a mere $30, Maria Gajewski can think of nothing but . . . 'a big fruit salad,' she said, smiling at the thought. 'Anything with color, flavor and vitamins looks really good to me right now.'"[9]

Gajewski ate a lot of brown and beige foods during that month: oatmeal, brown rice, lentils, pinto beans, peanut butter, macaroni, and wheat bread. So, while consuming an average of nearly 1,400 calories a day, she lost about eight pounds, but gained an understanding that having variety in your diet is a luxury we take for granted. "We get used to Chinese for dinner one night and pizza the next, but that's not how the rest of the world is," said Gajewski.

Let's ask Maria Gajewski: How much would you enjoy a slice of your favorite pizza? She answers: +10 happydons.

How can this be? We saw before that one slice of pizza gave 5 happydons. How is it possible to get 10 happydons if the happiness S-curve reads 5 on the positive side for one slice of pizza? But if we are consistent with our theory, we can see what has happened during Maria's ordeal. During periods of abstinence, one sustains consumption *below* the adaptation level (for food, this means an intake below 2,500 calories a day). Therefore, one builds up *negative* levels of satiation, which creates an unmet need. In the S-curve, recall that happiness is calculated as an increment from the satiation level. Therefore, when satiation levels are negative, one obtains a huge increase due to the steepness of the curve on the negative side. This craving—in mathematical terms—arises from the steepness of the S-curve for losses! In other words, craving follows from the combination of the third and fifth laws of happiness.

In our system, negative satiation levels build up if consumption below adaptation levels is sustained for a sufficient number of periods—in Gajewski's case, one month was certainly enough time. And negative satiation leads to craving.

Craving has been extensively studied in research on addictions. Craving is usually measured by self-reports of subjects on multi-item questionnaires.[10] Some researchers argue that craving arises because of an imbalance in brain activity that results from nonconsumption.[11] Empirical studies on craving usually focus on things like food, drugs, alcohol, and smoking. As you could probably guess, chocolate, for example, is the most craved food, especially among females.[12] Craving can be induced by environmental factors, such as the first sign of snow for a ski enthusiast, or the first warm days of spring for someone planning a summer at the beach. As we've all experienced, finally getting to the slopes or to the beach after craving those experiences for so long brings a great deal of pleasure. Thus, to experience high intensity of emotions we must suffer through some deprivation. For instance, after a very long hike in the cold weather, we really appreciate a warm shower, or after standing in a concert for a couple of hours, simply sitting down is a source of satisfaction.

Marketers use promotional tools, such as a brief stay in a luxury resort, to create desire. Similarly, an outing to celebrate an anniversary is made more enjoyable if we just go about our simple and routine life for a few days before the big event, avoiding extraordinary events.

The Law of Satiation implies that voluntary abstinence, which creates heightened need, maximizes the peak happiness experienced afterward, once consumption resumes. In India, for the eight days before Ashtami,[13] people will eat only austere food (fruit and water), and abstain from meat, fish, and the use of spices. Not using spices is particularly tough, as these people are used to spicy foods. On the day of Ashtami there is a big celebration with rich meals. Periods of abstinence followed by a period of celebration are common in religions, such as Ramadan for Muslims. These celebrations are particularly joyous.

When we incorporate satiation, our model predicts that the maximum satisfaction is obtained not immediately after the initial indulgence, but after abstaining for the right amount of time. For example, imagine that a friend of yours goes to a party tonight and falls madly in love at first sight. The lovers dance the night away, all the while staring adoringly into each other's eyes. They part reluctantly at night's end, each one eager to see the other as soon as possible. The question is, in order to maximize the happiness gained from their next meeting, when should they see each other again?

The laws of happiness would suggest that they shouldn't see each other the next day, since they will still be satiated from the night before. Nor should they wait too long, since the romance they've cultivated will dissipate and they'll reacclimate to their lives without the other. So, if possible, they should wait a few days and allow the craving to build up, and then they will each attain maximum joy from reuniting.

We realize we're being terribly unromantic here, treating true love like a slice of pizza or a round of golf. But, for better or worse, all these endeavors use the same mechanisms of adaptation, satiation, and craving to induce happiness in each of us.

CULTIVATE INTERESTS

If we have a wide variety of interests then we can move from one interest to another when we begin to feel monotony. Of course, too many interests may hamper their proper development, so there is an ideal balance between the number of interests we should cultivate and the amount of time available. People who take interest in a variety of activities seem generally happier than those who don't. If you enjoy watching sports, reading books, gardening, having meals with friends and family, engaging in outdoor activities, seeing new places, and getting to know new people, then much of your free time goes toward joyful activities. Contrary to a romantic view that hermits seem to lead trouble-free lives in their isolation, the fact remains that hermits do not lead happy lives. The popular cliché that variety is the spice of life is surprisingly valid.

But variety by itself is not a primary source of joy; rather it is the novelty and surprise produced by variety that is the main driver of joy. In a large meadow fertile with flowers in bloom, the variety is less noticed. In a land of rocky hills, a spring of wildflowers comes as an exquisite surprise. That's why most people appreciate the changing of seasons: the variety of the weather and the vegetation are new to the eyes, whereas in tropical lands the always-green scenery, while spectacular, may not be that exciting to someone who lives there year round.

Alas, our brain is so wired that novelty does give us pleasure. Recall the study of the monkeys. When the monkeys were offered raisins and not their customary apple, their neurons fired strongly in response to the welcome change.[14]

One thing we can do to improve our happiness is to seek out even the simplest novel experiences whenever possible. For example, recent studies have shown that married couples can rekindle their romance by trying new experiences together, which activate the same brain circuits that lit up when the couple first fell in love. So, although it might seem romantic to visit the same restaurant or beach resort for your anniversary every year, you'll actually be better off trying someplace new each time.

HAPPINESS IN ACTION

Every month try at least one thing you've never done, or haven't done in a long time. Try cooking a dish you've never made before, join a Tai Chi session in the local park, or fly a kite with your kids. It really doesn't matter what it is; it's the fact that it's a new experience that will make it memorable and generate happiness.

CHAPTER 8

The Sixth Law of Happiness

Presentism

> The great source of both the misery and disorders of human life, seems to arise from over-rating the difference between one permanent situation and another.
>
> —Adam Smith, *The Theory of Moral Sentiments*

You pull out the crumpled lottery ticket from your pocket and anxiously compare your ticket to the winning numbers. Your heart is pounding as you see that one number after another matches the winning numbers. You triple check until your mind fully grasps the fact that you have indeed won a million-dollar jackpot. You are in shock, but within a few minutes you are giddy with joy.

Now, stop jumping up and down and hugging complete strangers, and ask, "How happy will I be a year from now?" You will probably expect to be extremely happy. After all, your life has just changed dramatically for the better, right?

How good are we at predicting future happiness? To address this question, the psychologists Daniel Kahneman and Jackie Snell gave ice cream or yogurt of different flavors to a group of subjects for eight consecutive days. The subjects were asked to report their actual liking and their predicted liking. The most surprising result was that the actual liking and the predicted liking had a near zero correlation.[1]

A bias is a systematic error when making predictions. For instance, someone who is consistently optimistic about traffic conditions is biased. In forecasting happiness, there is one major bias that has multiple off-shoots.[2] The bias in predicting happiness is so prevalent that it assumes the status of a law:

> *The Sixth Law—Presentism: We forecast that future preferences and emotions will be more similar to our current preferences and emotions than they actually will be.*

People rarely take into account that their preferences are going to change. In fact, preferences and emotions change more than we think. When they are in a heightened emotional state, people do not imagine that their intense feelings of anger will dissipate quickly.

If you won the lottery, you would predict your future happiness based on your present euphoric state; but alas, your prediction would turn out to be too optimistic. If researchers are right, your happiness level a year from now will not be much different from what it was before winning the lottery. Unfortunately, your exuberance will not have the lasting power that you imagine it will.

Presentism makes us equally inept at predicting future unhappiness. Take depression as an example, a state of despair that feeds on itself. A depressed person expects to remain in that state for a long time. It is this dark vision of the future that reinforces the depression. But research shows that people usually recover from depression sooner than anticipated.

We are quite confident that a higher income, a promotion, or marrying our high school sweetheart will produce happiness. And of course, we predict that we will not engage in unsafe sex—it is only for those who lack self-control and are irresponsible. But in the heat of the moment, we are unable to resist temptation and do just the opposite of what we predicted. A recovering alcoholic or a gambler may overestimate the strength of his willpower. He may succumb to drinking or gambling once he steps into a bar or a casino.

We accurately predict that we will be mad if a restaurant overcharges us for a meal, sad if we fail a test, and disappointed if it rains during a beach vacation. Even in these adverse situations, our negative feelings do not last too long—even though at the very moment of the experience it seems as if they would linger forever. We tend to be correct when predicting the direction, positive or negative, of our emotional reactions. But we fail to predict correctly the duration and intensity of these reactions.

Romantic love is the prototypical example of an emotional state that we believe will last forever, as evidenced by the last line of so many romantic fairytales: "and they lived happily ever after." Research on human relationships shows that, rather than romantic love, sharing as many traits of character as possible (both extroverted and social or both introverted, both methodical or both spontaneous, both risk averse or both risk seeking) and common attitudes and values are better predictors of happiness in relationships. Shared character traits and similar attitudes minimize day-to-day conflict and make the relationship run smoothly.[3] We will never know if Romeo and Juliet would have lived a life of bliss together. More likely, they would have had ups and downs through raising a family and journeying through life, like most other couples. But love interrupted is a better story than love moderated by mundane living challenges over time.

We now explore some implications of presentism.

ADAPTATION BIAS

Recall that for many emotions, our mind produces happiness by comparing reality to some expectation. A particular form of presentism is to project the current expectation. This particular form of presentism is called *adaptation bias.* Because we think that expectations will not change much, we predict that future happiness is triggered by the difference between future reality and *current* expectation, that is:

PREDICTED HAPPINESS *equals*
FUTURE REALITY *minus* CURRENT EXPECTATIONS

In reality, expectations will change, and actual happiness will be triggered by the difference between future reality and *future* expectation, or:

ACTUAL HAPPINESS *equals*
FUTURE REALITY *minus* FUTURE EXPECTATIONS

Adaptation bias makes it difficult to imagine what it is like to be adapted to a better or to a worse life. We do recognize that life will return to normal after an adverse event, such as failed relationship, a job loss, or watching our favorite football team lose a big game. We underestimate how quickly this adjustment takes place, however. As the saying goes, "Time heals all wounds," and it usually does so even faster than we expect.

The most dramatic example is that of lottery winners who are happier, but not much so, a year after winning the lottery. Similarly, people who become paraplegics are almost completely adapted to their new situation one year after their loss. We adapt to both good and bad circumstances much faster than anticipated.

Adaptation bias is not a merely academic curiosity. It may influence life balance decisions. Most of us would love to have a beachfront house and a higher social status. There is indeed some happiness gain with these acquisitions. But, as we know, our expectations move up as well and we get adapted to a higher standard of living. The current perception of how great it would be to have a beach house, together with the inability to imagine ourselves adapted to it, makes us believe that the beach house will bring us much happiness. To support this desired lifestyle, we must work harder, and that takes time away from family, friends, and even sleep. There is therefore a gradual decline in leisure time, and total happiness, along with our health, may decline over time.

We are not suggesting that you should not improve your income and status. What we do suggest is that if you are not watchful you are likely to get caught up in a sinister game where your ambition for higher material well-being is likely to rob you of precious time for social relationships, family, and other community activities that do guarantee happiness.

Adaptation bias, the inability to see that our expectations will escalate, distorts our perception of the contribution that wealth and fame has on total happiness. The actress Michelle Pfeiffer observed: "I had achieved everything in the industry: fame, respect, awards, money, . . . even love. But I didn't have the essentials to value that treasure, I lacked time to enjoy and be with my family."

A harmonious balance between work and leisure is required to achieve a happy life. We believe that an awareness of adaptation bias will help you make better lifestyle choices and strike a proper balance between your personal and professional lives. Even Warren Buffett, the world's richest person, had to pause and rebalance his lifestyle to include bridge. If we were able to predict future adaptation levels accurately then the caution we prescribe would be unnecessary. Because of adaptation bias, we are likely to predict more happiness from improved material well-being than we will actually realize.

SATIATION BIAS

Do you have a tendency to buy more groceries when you are hungry? If yes, you are not alone. In a classic study, researchers gave some shoppers a muffin to eat and others not.[4] Those who had a muffin bought less than those who did not. Shoppers who are hungry tend to overbuy food. When hungry, we anticipate staying hungry, and when full, we also predict that we will stay full. After a heavy lunch, you do not want to even think about the menu for dinner, at least until you start to get hungry again.

Just as we found that our presentism causes us to have an adaptation bias (we think our expectations won't change), it also causes a "satiation bias," leading us to believe that the current satiation level will not change much.

Inducing overpurchasing when consumers have a low current level of satiation has been used as a marketing tool. For instance, at the beginning of the ski season, when people are "hungry" for skiing, they predict that they may go skiing more often than they actually will. Hence, they may buy that package deal for ten days of skiing. As the season unfolds and the satiation level for skiing increases, the consumer may end up not taking advantage of the package. Another all-too-familiar example is the discounted fitness membership frequently offered after the Christmas and New Year holidays. People buy into the seemingly good deal with the accompanying resolve to lose weight and get in shape for the upcoming year. The diligence of exercising generally wears off after a few weeks, and the discount membership ends up being a much better deal for the fitness club than for the member.

Xavi is a friend of ours who wanted to go kayaking. He told us that he planned a ten-day trip. We told him that, although he is now very eager to get into the kayak, in a few days he might become tired (satiated) of kayaking. In fact, Xavi listened to us and shortened the trip to six days. In the actual vacation, after four days of kayaking, Xavi had had enough of paddling and spent the last two days of vacation reading. Next time you purchase vacation days on a cruise ship or resort, make sure you anticipate the satiation associated with staying in the same place for several days!

REPEATED PROCRASTINATION

In a classic study, children were placed in a room by themselves and told that they could call the experimenter by ringing a bell.[5] They were told that they would receive a small piece of candy if they immediately summoned the experimenter. If, however, they waited for the experimenter to return, say in fifteen minutes, then they would receive a large piece of candy. Some children would rather have the immediate reward and sacrifice the delayed reward of a larger piece of candy. Other preferred to wait for the large piece of candy. Those who waited apparently were more successful in life. Here, we focus on another finding. When the candy was displayed, children found it harder to wait. Presentism explains this finding because the sight and smell of the candy increased the desire for the candy, and the present emotions guided the decision making.

Presentism, giving too much importance to the emotion of the moment, causes people to behave myopically and opt for immediate gratification even if they know that a delay is in their long-term interest. We have all experienced the pull of "sleeping in" when we reach out to shut off the alarm clock. After all, the discomfort of waking up is immediate and the benefits of being in the office earlier are remote.

Recent research suggests that our brains react differently when considering immediate or delayed rewards. The limbic system, which reacts to emotions and is myopic, becomes active when people choose immediate rewards. The lateral prefrontal cortex, which is a more deliberative system that weighs present and future rewards, reacts when delayed rewards are chosen. Recognizing that the allure of an immediate reward may be too tempting, we can design control mechanisms to overcome this bias. We can place the alarm clock away from the bed. It will be annoying having to stagger to it in the morning, but we will not be late to the office. Truck drivers use a device that sounds an alarm when drowsiness causes their grip on the steering wheel to loosen.

The following example illustrates the effect of presentism when it comes to decisions over time.

> *Think about your favorite flavor of ice cream. Say it is raspberry. Would you rather have one scoop of raspberry ice cream now, or wait one week and get two scoops?*
>
> *Now consider a second situation. Would you rather wait four weeks and get one scoop of raspberry ice cream, or wait five weeks and get two scoops?*

Because of presentism, some people would prefer one scoop now, rather than wait one week and get two scoops. In the second situation, the same people may prefer to wait five weeks and get two scoops. What this implies is that people may say today that they prefer two scoops in five weeks, but as time passes, and the one scoop of ice cream becomes an immediate possibility, they fall into the temptation and settle for the immediate and smaller reward.

Marketers know about presentism, and exploit it to sell more. Consumers are attracted to "buy now, pay later" products even when financial conditions are not very favorable. Many consumers are attracted by advertisements offering mobile phones for extraordinarily low prices—many times they're actually free. However, the variable cost of each call is often more expensive than for other plans. Most people would rather buy a cheaper electrical appliance even though it will use substantially more electricity or require more expensive maintenance over its lifetime. Presentism is exacerbated by high arousal states. People engage in unprotected sex in spite of the high cost of catching diseases such as AIDS. "Just say no" is a good slogan and works if sufficient conviction is built; otherwise, deciding to carry a contraceptive may be a more effective solution for avoiding unwanted pregnancies.

Getting addicted to alcohol, smoking, gambling, drugs, and other bad habits may ruin our lives. The force of the emotion of the moment is strong, and choosing impulsively may bring disaster. It is more prudent to take steps to avoid the impulse of the moment. Ulysses plugged the ears of his sailors with wax and bound himself to the mast, and safely sailed past the Sirens' island. Countless other sailors, enchanted by the Sirens' songs, perished on the rocks around their island.

How much of the future I can feel in the present depends on the magnitude of the consequences. It is easy to joyfully anticipate an adventurous trip three months before taking off. In contrast, moderate events such as a dinner with friends or attending a play do not produce much joy of anticipation until some days before the event. In other words, the smaller the consequences in the future, the more we discount future happiness or unhappiness.

It is common nowadays to sell consumer products on credit with an emphasis on monthly payments that obscure the total cost. Some marketers frame the purchase price in the form of daily payments; "For just three dollars a day you could enjoy all the benefits of a health club." As each payment seems tiny, it makes consumers believe that the product is affordable.

A professor in the college of a British university died suddenly without leaving a will. On investigation, he turned out to have had a large estate. In his room was a form to bequest money to the college, which he had not filled in. Presumably filling in the form the following day always appeared to be the better option. As the professor had no close family, the money eventually went to a distant relative, and not to the university as presumably he wished.

We're all familiar with the saying, "Why put off until tomorrow what you can do today?" It seems like a simple enough edict to follow, and yet so many of us regularly ignore its wisdom and procrastinate over and over again. Procrastination is a consequence of how presentism distorts the perception of doing an onerous task whose benefits will be received in the future. The future benefits do not suffer from a small delay. What is the big deal if I sign this will today or tomorrow, or do this computer backup today or tomorrow? The net effect of this distorted calculation is that doing onerous things tomorrow always seems like a good idea. One ironic consequence of presentism is failing to see that tomorrow we will procrastinate again. And this is the trap.

LISTEN TO YOUR HEART: EMOTIONS ARE "SMART"

> It is only with the heart that one can see rightly; what is essential is invisible to the eye.
> —Antoine de Saint-Exupéry

Although we may have a tendency to exaggerate the emotion of the moment, we should not ignore such emotions. Emotions, which need not be rational, have intelligence hidden in them (it may sound curious, but our brain naturally tries to make sense of everything, even our laughs and sobs). We feel them for a reason. Emotions and feelings are designed to predict happiness in the near future. In many instances, "follow your heart" turns out to be a very good idea! Malcolm Gladwell's book, *Blink,* argues that intuitive decision making often beats more analytic approaches that ignore emotions.[6] Of course, he also shows examples where trained intuition does even better.

The brain researcher Antonio Damasio is famous for showing that individuals unable to feel emotions are very poor decision makers, as they cannot sense the consequences of their actions.[7] In the words of David Hume, "Reason is, and only ought to be, the slave of the Passions." And these passions are the engine for all our deeds. Without these drives we would be inert and unable to act, or even reason.

Often, the inner voice points to the right path. Physical pain, for instance, indicates that something is wrong with the body. If you accidentally touch a hot stove, the pain triggers a quick withdrawal of the hand. Conversely, pleasure is a signal to seek something out; we continue to eat calorie-rich foods because we enjoy the taste.

Negative emotions are part of our lives and no one can claim to have lived a fully human life if he or she has not gone through some emotional darkness. Negative emotions, ironically, are often there to show us the way to happiness. Sadness, for instance, may be a sign to society that we need a little extra help. And loneliness motivates us to leave the comfort of our home to seek a social life, eventually finding friends with whom we manage to establish lasting relationships that bring us happiness.

Emotions can provide a strong drive for change. Romantic love, for example, is sufficiently intense and lasting that it can compel us, effortlessly, to undergo dramatic changes. How many love stories are there in which people turned their lives upside-down in order to be closer to their beloved?

Emotions also have social intelligence. Very likely, if you feel that you've been treated unfairly, you will get angry and seek to punish the offender and demand justice, even if you get hurt yourself.

Hercules was the greatest hero of Greece. He was the strongest man on Earth and could not be defeated by any earthly power. His emotions were quickly aroused and were often out of control, however. In a rage, he killed his wife and children. He even threatened to shoot the sun with an arrow because he was too hot. He was a noble soul, so he paid for his misdeeds by voluntarily accepting punishments. His penance, called "the labors of Hercules," consisted of twelve tasks, each one difficult and dangerous. On occasion he punished himself even when others had agreed to exonerate him.

Hercules would have been a perfect hero had he used his reason to control his fury. He could have avoided the sorrows that followed him for the wrongs he did in his rages.

The emotion of the moment may alert us to an impending danger but it may also lead us toward a myopic action. Therefore, the heart sometimes has to be moderated, and even overruled, by the head.

FIGHTING PRESENTISM

If you convince yourself of the reality of presentism, then having more self-control and choosing ways that indeed will make you happier becomes easier.

Here are four recommendations to cope with presentism.

1. ***Rely on the direct experience of others:*** Rather than speculating about how much happiness some product or experience will generate, you would be better off asking a friend who already owns that product or who has enjoyed that experience. If your friend tells you that visiting a certain city or country is really wonderful, you'll probably feel the same way.[8]

2. ***Stick to the original plan.*** Suppose you have made some plan; let's call it plan A. For example, plan A is to attend a conference on Saturday. But when Saturday arrives, you feel like skipping the conference and staying at home to watch a sports event. This is plan B.

   Which of the two is better, plan A or plan B? Plan A may be best because at some point it made sense. Plan B may be best because it is what we feel like doing at the moment. In view of the law of presentism, our recommendation is: Stick to the original plan. If you always do that, more often than not you will find that A is indeed better. On a few occasions you may realize that plan B would have been better. That doesn't matter. Keep sticking to the original plan. If you do, over time you will better know your preferences, without the confusion created by changing plans, and will improve your judgment when choosing the original plan.

3. ***Willpower.*** It has been found that willpower, like muscles, increases with exercise, although it also weakens if we are required to use willpower continuously for an extended period of time. The Stanford marketing professor Baba Shiv designed a clever experiment to observe the role of the heart and of the mind in decision making.[9] The key idea is to induce *cognitive load,* that is, burden people's minds so that they use them less! Here is how the experiment works: Half the people in the experiment were asked to remember an eight-digit number (high cognitive load). The other half were asked to remember a three-digit number (low cognitive load). Next, they had to choose between a fruit salad and a chocolate bar. Well, it turned out that more subjects in the eight-digit group chose the chocolate bar, compared to the subjects in the three-digit group. Under high cognitive load, the head is busier and it releases control to the heart (or intuition). Although a judicious choice would be the fruit salad (think long term, avoid overeating), the emotion of

the moment recommends the chocolate bar (calories are good, chocolate tastes good, take it now). So next time you want your guests to taste the delicious cake you have prepared for them, simply ask them to remember a phone number, or offer them the cake while they are trying to solve a Sudoku!

4. *Regulate the emotion of the moment.* If you want to diet, for example, you may want to imagine that a piece of chocolate cake is made out of mud. This thought will easily keep you from eating the cake. Another possibility to avoid the emotion of the moment controlling us is to fool ourselves. To do so, we promise ourselves that we will give in to the temptation at some future time. For example, it is easier to wake up on time if we promise ourselves that we will take a nap later. Or when we see this fancy smartphone or motorcycle that we suddenly desire, we can convince ourselves that we will buy this item next year. When the time comes, other matters will occupy our minds and we will have easily overcome the temptation.

HAPPINESS IN ACTION

Realize the many different ways in which presentism affects your life. Go on with the long-planned bike ride with your children or an outing with your friends this weekend. We all have a tendency to postpone our diet and exercise plan because we are too occupied with our work today. Remind yourself that "tomorrow never comes" and today is the best day to begin your diet and exercise plan.

PART III

Engineering a Happier Life

CHAPTER 9

The Treasure of Happiness

Basic Goods

The man is the richest whose pleasures are the cheapest.
—Henry David Thoreau

In 1978, researchers at the University of Connecticut presented a group of adults with a list of twenty-four big-ticket consumer items such as cars, houses, and swimming pools. First the research subjects were asked how many of these items they already possessed and then they were asked the following question: "When you think of the good life—the life you'd like to have—which of the things on the list, if any, are part of the good life as far as you are personally concerned?"[1]

There were no big surprises in the results, which showed that people thought that they needed more things than they already had to live the good life. In fact, respondents between twenty-five and forty-four years old owned an average of 2.5 items from the list, but the ideal according to them was an average of 4.3 items.

Sixteen years later, the same people were interviewed once again. At that point, they owned a greater number of items from the list, so they must have considered themselves closer to the good life, right? Well, given what you now know about adaptation, you already know the answer.

As if they were running on a treadmill, people now needed more in order to think themselves closer to the good life, On average, the number of items they now felt they needed to own had increased to 5.4.[2]

The conclusion from this study is that new material aspirations arise as previous ones are satisfied, making all of us work harder and harder to see ourselves in exactly the same situation all over again: wanting something new. This is the nature of adaptive and conspicuous goods.

Recent research on materialism suggests that excessive concern with consumer goods and material possessions is inversely related to positive developmental outcomes.[3] In her study of the social psychology of material possessions, Helga Dittmar of the University of Sussex shows that once people find out that material things won't satisfy their happiness, they are disappointed and even less happy than they were beforehand.[4]

Our expectations for consumption are like the carbon dioxide levels in the atmosphere: once they increase beyond a certain point, it is very difficult to make them decrease. We face a sort of emotional "global warming"; if we get used to consuming too much too soon, our future happiness is put at risk. One typical example is that of the children of wealthy parents who are not able to keep up with the lifestyle they've always known.

Adaptive goods can deliver happiness, but only if we choose a less-to-more pattern of consumption. But unfortunately, presentism interferes with our ability to implement crescendo strategies in life choices. In practice, adaptive goods are an unreliable source of happiness, making us vulnerable to disappointment. A similar difficulty arises with conspicuous goods, those that give happiness based on comparison to others. Why would we put our happiness in the hands of our neighbors, since we have so little control over their consumption habits?

Given our difficulties dealing with adaptation and social comparison, is happiness possible? Is there an easy and foolproof way to be happy? In this and the following two chapters, we will explore three types of goods and activities that deliver assured happiness. That is, they defy the Law of Adaptation, but in different ways. Let's begin with the first type: basic goods.

BASIC GOODS

Can you remember the last time you dusted off those old photo albums you have stashed away somewhere? Take another look at those pictures and see if you can figure out what really makes you happy. In which moments were you smiling contently? Perhaps it was during that birthday party when all your friends came over and you had a fun time hanging out eating strawberry pie together, or maybe it was that hot summer evening when you spent hours chatting over the dinner table with old friends about dozens of different topics involving people you have known for ages.

Spending time with friends and family, eating croissants and drinking coffee on Sunday morning, and listening to music you haven't heard for a long time are all examples of goods that can consistently make us happy—and are not subject to adaptation or social comparison.

In 2006, a McDonald's employee in Wales won a lottery jackpot of almost two million dollars. Eighteen months later he was back at his previous job, saying that he missed his workmates.[5] He told the BBC: "I must be the luckiest man alive—not only did I win a fortune but my wife understands the importance of football and now I've got my old job back." Even after winning a huge amount of money, he still went to work every day—a wise decision that will pay off with increasing happiness, as he still trusts in his old lifestyle to deliver happiness.

Basic goods, such as food, are subject to all our laws of happiness: we experience diminishing sensitivity and they produce satiation, we experience negative emotions (hunger) if our consumption of them is below some reference level, and pleasure if our consumption is above the reference level. What makes basic goods special is our second law. For basic goods there is little or no adaptation, and they are not subject to social comparison. The expectations or base of comparison changes very little. Therefore, happiness is independent of our past consumption (except for satiation effects) and of the indulgences of others. If adaptive and conspicuous goods are relative, basic goods are absolute.

Therefore, basic goods can be consumed at a constant rate over time with no need to plan for a less-to-more strategy. The only thing to keep in mind is the satiation associated with basic goods. Consequently, as long as we ensure sufficient variety and space out our consumption of them sufficiently, basic goods will deliver happiness for sure.

If we were trying to sell basic goods, the advertising should read something along the lines of "satisfaction guaranteed," because no matter how much you get from it, it still has the power to make you smile in the very same way.

Think back to a day when you were really hungry when you got home and rushed to the kitchen to put something in your stomach—the cold piece of chicken from yesterday's lunch tasted delicious, didn't it? Basic goods are like this all the time; they always make you happy!

But it's not just food that makes the basic goods wonder-list. The economist Tibor Scitovsky argues that cultural goods, such as music, literature, and art, are less subject to hedonic adaptation than "comfort" goods, such as homes and cars.[6]

To clarify the difference between adaptive and basic goods, let's look at the following example. Your boss decides to give you some time off for your good performance. You are free to use the next month's Friday afternoons as you wish. If your objective is to maximize happiness, which of the following two options would you choose?

1. Get a freelance project. Since you're working the rest of the week, keeping busy a few more hours won't make that much difference, and with the extra money you can purchase a fancy portable GPS for your car.

2. Accept a friend's invitation to join a group of former classmates who get together every Friday afternoon to attend salsa dance classes, and later go out for drinks to practice some new moves.

Let's apply the laws of happiness and see which choice produces the most happiness. With the first option, your expectations rise as you think about how nice the new GPS system would look in your car. After you buy it, you enjoy a short-lived burst of happiness. Adaptation begins right away, and your happiness soon decays to the level it was before you began.

The second option, taking salsa dancing lessons with friends, is safer. Friendship, as a basic good, always delivers. Therefore, your enjoyment derived from this experience is more durable and it yields happiness Friday after Friday.

The additional income acquired by working harder for a few weeks may be OK, but the problem is that the pattern will likely repeat. After the GPS system, you may crave a new flat-panel TV or a fancy stereo system. You could find yourself wanting to take on other freelance projects to sustain this adaptive consumption even after the month of free Friday afternoons has expired.

BOOSTING YOUR SMILE FREQUENCY

How can we tell whether a good is adaptive or not? Here's a quick test. Bring to your mind some good or activity, which we will call X.
Is X a basic good?
Ask yourself the following questions:

1. If nobody knew I'm buying or experiencing X, would I still want X?
2. Will I enjoy X in the future, say five years from now, as much as I do now?

If the answer is yes to both, then X is basic!

Let's say that on your way home you walk past a popcorn stand, the smell of melted butter on the popcorn is delicious and your craving for the popcorn is translated into the enormous satisfaction you can reliably anticipate once you start eating it. So, you buy a bag and eat the whole thing before you get home.

A few weeks later on the same route home, you find yourself in the same situation and you buy and enjoy the buttered popcorn once again. Would you classify the buttered popcorn as a basic good?

Food is the most straightforward example of a basic good. It is a major source of happiness for human beings—obviously, hunger enhances the pleasure of taste—but hunger due to a lack of food or surfeit as a result of gluttony are both sources of distress. People who eat the right kind of food in the right amount at the right time enjoy not only the good taste but also the health benefits associated with it. Meals eaten with others are both nutritional and social, so there are both "anticipated" and "remembered" pleasures associated with such events.

Although food is a basic good, there are also some foods for which we experience adaptation. Think of chili pepper, coffee, or beer: you probably didn't like them the very first time you tried them, but now you enjoy dishes seasoned with chili pepper, and you probably enjoy coffee or beer.

In the same way we have basic goods, we also have basic bads. Those are activities or consumption for which we obtain permanent unhappiness, and expectations do not adapt over time. Basic goods and basic bads are different sides of the same coin, as they are based on mechanisms of our emotional map that are not adaptive.

There are three categories of basic goods and bads that pass the test: the needs of the body, the needs of the heart, and the needs of the mind.

> The needs of the body: food, health, shelter, sex, and rest. Their lack produces pain, in its multiple forms.
>
> The needs of the heart: company, connection, love, and belonging. Their lack produces loneliness.
>
> The needs of the mind: peace, safety, trust, hope, beauty, and understanding. Their lack produces fear and anxiety.

NEEDS OF THE BODY

Normally we tend to think of health as a very important factor in our lives. Good health does not make us happy, but the lack of it—especially chronic pain or discomfort—can indeed lower our happiness. Most people take good health for granted and overlook the fact that being in good shape helps them avoid much unhappiness. In our language, the reference level is set at a healthy condition. It is a blessing that modern medicine has been able to mitigate pain in many of its forms.

Certain health limitations, if not accompanied by pain, are adaptive. A good example is paraplegia. Studies done on people who suffer debilitating injuries that cause them to require wheelchairs show that right after the accident their happiness levels, not surprisingly, go down. But only a year later, they come back to almost the same happiness set point they had before their accident![7]

As with health, we can easily imagine that a lack of other basic goods such as food or shelter will produce persistent unhappiness. And yet we often take these things for granted and don't appreciate their positive impact on our lives.

Sex is perhaps the most intense and pleasurable experience for humans. It is no surprise that, in a survey, sex is rated the highest on pleasure among all activities. Average happiness during sex is rated 4.7 out of 5. The next highest rated activity is eating, which is rated 4 out of 5. The role of sex in the propagation of the species is obvious. We argued earlier that emotions are "smart." They alert us to impending dangers or forthcoming rewards. Sexual desire is similarly smart. There is something to be said about the chemistry and initial attraction between two people; love at first sight is not an exaggeration. But we also said earlier that the head must sometimes keep the heart in check. In the selection of a potential mate, the instinct may be right, but a bit of thought before one says "I do" may help ensure a long-term stable relationship. Even Darwin wrote down the pros and cons of whether to marry. Both heart and head told him to marry Emma, with whom he ended up having ten children.

Hunger, thirst, and sex are the most basic and primitive urges that shake the pleasure centers of our brains. During sex and especially at the point of orgasm the brain areas of intense pleasure become highly active. The brain areas for danger and worry—like the amygdala—are turned off. According to researchers, the key difference between men and women in reaching sexual satisfaction is that women need to trust their partner in order for the brain's danger and alert center to be deactivated.

We will call food, water, and sexual relations basic goods. Personal relations and helping others (charity) are basic goods as well. It is no wonder that the same parts of the brain light up when a person thinks of a charitable act as when his hunger or sexual desire is satisfied.

If sex is a source of heightened pleasure, then why are monks, who are celibate, so happy? Our seismogram of happiness explains this apparent paradox. Monks derive all their joy from eating, sleeping, socializing, and spiritual activities. Furthermore, they have modest expectations and live in the relatively low-stress environment of a monastery. So their happiness seismogram does not dip below the zero line too frequently and they maintain a relatively constant, but high, level of happiness above the zero line. Yes, indeed they may not experience the pleasure that sexual activity provides, but they accrue a higher net total of positive minus negative emotions than the typical person navigating life in modern society.

NEEDS OF THE HEART

If you were meditating and wanted to go, in your mind, to your "happy place," where would that be? Maybe you would imagine an isolated tropical beach, an untouched ski slope, or a beautiful Tuscan hillside. In reality, though, you would probably enjoy greater and longer lasting happiness much closer to home, among family and friends.

The sociologist Ruut Veenhoven and his team have collected happiness data from ninety-one countries, representing two-thirds of the world's population. He has concluded that Denmark is home to the happiest people in the world, with Switzerland close behind.[8]

The top-ranking countries have long democratic traditions, where men and women enjoy the same rights under stable governments—Switzerland, for instance, with its referendum system, in which citizens have a say in issues in addition to electing political decision makers.

Interestingly enough, one of the more detailed points of the research found that 92 percent of the people in Denmark are members of some sort of group, ranging from sports to cultural interests. To avoid loneliness, we must seek active social lives, maintain friendships, and enjoy stable relationships.

The American social worker Sandy Cartlidge is very aware that her bridge group is a source of good fun. Every Wednesday evening she meets with three other women to drink some wine and chat over a few hands of bridge.

> The passion my friends and I have for bridge combined with the fun we all have together is indeed a reason to smile. Bridge and my friends are two of the most important aspects of my life and I never fail to have a wonderful time when I am with my bridge friends. We travel to the coast and mountains for two or three days for getaways and of course get together and play in each other's homes. Food and wine is another important aspect of our time together. We share our lives with each other, the happy, sad, disappointing, and joyous occasions of our lives. We know each other very well and each other's families. We celebrate the lives of our children together and most of us work together, so we have the passion of our work that we need to process and discuss at times. The game of bridge itself is a very mentally challenging and ever-changing one that can be played seriously or for fun. We of course are the "fun" group and never take ourselves too seriously.

How would you predict whether someone is happy? The best general factor to predict happiness, it turns out, is that individual's number and quality of social relationships.

Indeed people are happier while in the presence of others. What makes a good community is the trust among its members. By means of personality tests, psychologists have found that people who are more concerned with their communities than with their material possessions are happier, and that social well-being correlates with interpersonal trust.[9]

NEEDS OF THE MIND

Over the years, we have accumulated so much knowledge about the world around us. The knowledge we have about particles and planets, plants and animals, and ourselves is astonishing. News about the discovery of water on Mars or that all blue-eyed people are linked by a single genetic mutation that occurred about ten thousand years ago piques our curiosity. With new technologies, we all have access to entertaining knowledge such as the TED talks given by experts, or entire TV channels devoted to animal life, history, and science. These can stimulate our minds and arouse our curiosity.

Epicurus assigned higher importance to pleasures of the mind than to pleasures of the body. For him, the ideal state of the soul is "tranquility," in the absence of fear and pain.[10] Peace of mind not only brings tranquility but also has positive effects on health and well-being. Jon Kabat-Zinn in his book *Full Catastrophe Living* explains how to achieve peace of mind through mindful meditation.[11] Mindful meditation has positive effects on stress reduction, physical health, and recovery from illness and injury. Kabat-Zinn has shown, for example, that meditation helps heal people with psoriasis (a skin disease), improves antibody response in our immune system, and even creates more activity in the brain toward cheerfulness.

For many, time spent in religious practices brings peace of mind and hope to the heart. Several studies have found a positive correlation between religious practice and happiness. This effect goes above and beyond what one would expect from the social support associated with belonging to a cohesive church community.[12]

In *Anatomy of an Illness as Perceived by the Patient*, Norman Cousins, an adjunct professor of medical humanities at the University of California, Los Angeles, documented in detail his own recovery from a degenerative collagen disease using laughter therapy. It seems that even in the face of life-threatening disease, positive emotions induced by humor and cheerfulness help the healing process. Negative emotions can produce negative biochemical changes in the body. Voodoo works that way. The voodoo doctor does not kill the person; the person kills himself. Cousins wrote, "Every person who is ill comes to the doctor with two diseases, not one. One is the disease that is diagnosed. The other is a powerful disease that goes by the name of panic."[13] By focusing on positive attitudes (love, hope, faith, laughter, the will to live, creativity, playfulness, purpose, joyousness, determination) we can induce our brains to produce beneficial biochemical changes in the body.

As we have seen throughout this chapter, the extent to which we can acknowledge and appreciate the basic goods in our lives (which, by the way, are all around us all the time), the greater happiness we will experience today and every day in the future.

HAPPINESS IN ACTION

The great thing about basic goods is that you don't have to hold back; you can indulge in them over and over again and they'll always deliver. So, for example, there's no need to hold off purchasing that comfortable new mattress to help you get a good night's sleep. Rest is a basic good, and you'll always appreciate it. Or, take a moment to appreciate a simple meal with your family. Try eating mindfully, really concentrating on the experience and appreciating the meal.

CHAPTER 10

Cumulative Comparison

We must cultivate our own garden.   —Voltaire

A traveler came upon a group of three hard-at-work stonemasons. He asked each in turn what he was doing. The first said, "I am sanding down this block of marble." The second said, "I am preparing a foundation." The third said, "I am building a cathedral." It is the third mason who saw his work as a task that would stay. As construction on the cathedral progresses, his happiness will continue to increase.

Carol Ryff of the University of Wisconsin distinguishes between "hedonic well-being," which are our feelings and mood in general, and "eudaimonic well-being," which involves having a purpose in life, continued personal growth, and good relationships with others.[1] Many other philosophers and thinkers have made this distinction between a pleasant life and a meaningful life. We have shown so far that our laws of happiness will help you build a pleasant life. We now investigate how the same laws can help you build a meaningful life.

Suppose that when engaged in an activity, you feel that your efforts are being accumulated, like the mason's stones that get "stored" in the walls of a cathedral. Or when learning a new language, each new word becomes part of your vocabulary. Those activities then accumulate in a bucket. Recall the fundamental equation: emotions are triggered by the comparison between reality and expectations. What distinguishes cumulative activities is the "reality" part of the equation. In cumulative activities, the reality part of the equation is the total effort accumulated so far, that is, the total water stored in the bucket. The bucket is the cathedral, the set of words we have learned so far, or the memories of all the trips we have taken. For noncumulative goods (adaptive, basic, and conspicuous), reality is the amount of activity done today, the stones that we placed today, or the water that we poured in the bucket today. The difference is subtle but critical.

When you fill a bucket with water using a hose, you can choose to watch the *stream* of water pouring into the bucket. Every day, some gallons of water enter the bucket, and you can focus on those gallons. In the bucket, you'll see the *stock* or total amount of water. The stream may be constant, but the level of water keeps increasing. The relationship between the stream and the stock is simple: the stock is the accumulation of the stream. If we consider the bucket, then we automatically get an increasing pattern.[2]

Now, consider table 1.

The first column represents a less goal-directed process. The second column represents accumulated actions. Even if the stream pours at a constant rate, there is an ongoing increase because water continues to accumulate in the bucket.

Our point here is that these goods that "fill us up" also follow the fundamental equation. *If reality is stored, then emotions can be triggered by the comparison between the stored levels of reality minus the expectation over these stored levels.*

HAPPINESS *equals*
ACCUMULATED REALITY *minus* SHIFTING
EXPECTATIONS

For cumulative goods and activities, emotions are triggered by the comparison between the *amount stored* and a *reference level* or expectation. The law of motion of expectations works the same way, that is, expectations chase the accumulated level of reality.

TABLE I

Viewing Reality as Cumulative

Stream (water poured today) IT DOES NOT COUNT	Stock (water stored in the bucket) IT COUNTS
Disconnected Actions	*Progress toward a Goal*
Job Study Activity Practicing sports Playing an instrument	Career Earning a degree Project Building skills Accumulating learning
Disconnected Emotions	*Life Narrative*
Joys and sorrows Entertainment sex Caring for a child	Part of the book of life Building a relationship Raising a family
Consumption	*Accumulation*
Keeping a gadget Buying a souvenir Profit	Collecting Adding this to a collection Net worth

Felipe is a very productive researcher. Lately, he has been publishing three papers per year in good research journals. In the current year, however, he has only managed to publish two papers. Is he happy or disappointed? You might predict that he is disappointed, because his productivity has decreased. If Felipe looks at his research career in a cumulative way, however, he will realize that he has moved from a total of twelve papers to fourteen. This thought makes him happy; every paper counts!

If Felipe takes a "stream" view of reality, then he will compare his current output with that of the previous years. But if Felipe takes a "bucket" view of reality, then he will compare his current total output of fourteen papers with the previous year's total output of twelve. Both in the "stream" view and in the "bucket" view, the base of comparison trails reality. But in the bucket viewpoint, the new paper always brings happiness, because the reality of having published fourteen papers is above the reference level of twelve.

If expectations chase reality, when considering goods as accumulating, will expectations also catch up with reality and bring happiness to zero? The answer is yes if we stop accumulating, but no if we maintain a constant rate of accumulation. As the bucket is being filled, perhaps at a constant rate, accumulated reality keeps increasing. Expectations will always trail this cumulative reality, but not sufficiently fast as to be able to catch up. Cumulative goods have the property that when consumed at a constant rate, we automatically create a crescendo (less-to-more) effect. And crescendo, as we well know, is what produces a constant flow of happiness, because it opens a continuous gap between reality and expectations.

In hindsight, the equation of accumulation is commonly present in the language we normally use. Albert is a former student of ours. He got married about two years ago and recently had his first child. During our conversation on happiness, he said: "You know, I went through some years of hippie life, but that life did not fill me up." And, commenting on a friend who constantly finds herself in unstable relationships, a relative noted, "She surely has a good time, but she does not build up."

Gardening is a good example of a cumulative activity. Mary enjoys gardening. At the beginning of each growing season, Mary spends her time preparing the soil and planting flowers and vegetables. In the ensuing weeks, Mary watches her plants grow from tiny seedlings to mature plants. Her levels of happiness are steady, as she does not get used to the change: the flower buds appear and the garden gradually blooms with beautiful colors and scents. For happiness, make sure your hobbies have as many cumulative aspects as possible.

Another example of a cumulative activity is a pilgrimage. In Europe there is a traditional pilgrimage to the Cathedral of Santiago de

Compostela in northern Spain. This is known as the Camino de Santiago. You are given a card at the start of the walk and your steps are tracked by the card, which gets stamped at destinations along the route. Some friends who got lost for a while during the camino were disappointed because "the extra steps taken while lost did not count." This shows the idea that steps that do not follow the camino do not accumulate, and therefore don't produce happiness. In fact, the physical experience during the camino is marked by blistered feet, exhaustion, hunger, and thirst. Walking in the countryside may sound romantic, but the reality is that the path may be nasty and the scenery is often not all that spectacular. The prospect of getting closer to the destination, socializing with the people you meet during the day, eating well-deserved meals, and getting much-needed sleep fills the mind with positive emotions. The experience itself becomes a cumulative good, a permanent deposit.

To find meaning in life, one needs to consume goods that either are cumulative or can be represented as cumulative in one's mind. A stamp collector probably sees the acquisition of a new stamp as a further accomplishment in building his entire collection, rather than as just acquiring a single new stamp.

Strong group identities such as those created by nations, sport teams, religious communities, charity organizations, and environmental conservation groups may be seen as buckets that store individual efforts. Therefore, people who identify with these causes see their effort and support being stored in that particular bucket, like a bank safe.

We want to contribute to things that last, or accumulate—think of the millions of dollars people donate to political campaigns or religious organizations. In fact, people will donate more to the construction of a hospital than to finance the operating expenses of the hospital.[3] Why should a dollar spent on a brick count more than a dollar donated to buy disposable gloves? The reason is simple: the brick will stay and give the donor a sense of contributing to a lasting cause.

A key characteristic of competent business leaders is the ability to provide a vision, a way to make sure that the collective efforts are progressing toward a meaningful goal that will be stored.

There are two important types of cumulative activities: goals and relationships. Before discussing these, let's try to understand better the positive and negative side of cumulative goods.

THE TWO SIDES OF THE COIN

Cumulative goods and basic goods act very similarly. Both basic and cumulative goods are solid ways to obtain a nice stream of happiness over and over. You set a challenging goal, and, here it is, you become engaged and happy! You begin a relationship, and, here it is, a stream of nice emotions begins flowing! As with basic goods, the optimal way to consume cumulative goods is approximately a constant rate.

If the accumulation process stops because we reach the goal or master the learning of some skill, then the happiness seismogram returns to the neutral level, as the expectations will eventually catch up with the accumulated level of reality.

The big drawback of basic goods is that their list is short. Cumulative goods have almost the same properties as basic goods, and their list is much longer, almost unlimited. This is the bright side of the coin. But there is a dark side that we should be aware of.

There is one important difference between cumulative goods and basic goods. In some cases, cumulative goods are permanent (the papers published, the goals attained). But in other occasions, the bucket where the cumulative good is stored can be broken and the goods stored can be lost. And here is where a huge loss is felt, because the new reality is zero, and the expectations are the bucket level before it was broken.

What if someone steals our MP3 player while we are walking down the street with all those songs recorded, each of which represents a unique moment? Indeed, if the collection of music is gone, if the deposit disappears, we suffer a great loss. All this joy that we had accumulated building the collection suddenly disappears. The same happens if we lose the trust of a friend.

The loss of cumulative goods has negative effects in several spheres of our lives. For many, the profession represents the most important goal in life. Their efforts are stored in a bucket called career. In the middle of a successful professional life, someone who loses a job and, therefore, finds himself unemployed suffers a great deal of dissatisfaction and unhappiness. Most of the unhappiness comes from seeing that the career bucket has been damaged or broken.

American surveys found that although 30 percent of the general population described themselves to be "very happy," only 11 percent of people without a job were "very happy."[4] According to the social psychologist Michael Argyle, the unemployed are normally bored, with very low self-esteem. Work is far from being just a source of money; it has actually been proven to be good for our happiness.

It's important to note that *not working* is different than being unemployed. For instance, retired people actually rate themselves high on happiness. Their career bucket did not break; it just stop being filled. In Britain, 36 percent of retired men and 35 percent of retired women felt very pleased. In contrast, 23 percent of employed men and 17 percent of employed women felt the same way.[5] Retired people say, however, that they miss their coworkers and the feeling of being useful.

For cumulative goods, the happiness seismograph may show four distinct phases.

1. Cumulative goods create a flow of happiness while they accumulate.

2. Once the accumulation process stops, happiness returns to a neutral level.

3. If the cumulative good is lost, then we experience unhappiness. Over time, we revert to neutral levels.

4. Happiness can be recovered by restarting the process of accumulation.

These four phases do not need to be experienced if, for example, the cumulative good is never lost. But potentially the four phases could occur.

Loss of a cumulative good produces great unhappiness. Losing a job, the breakup of a long-term relationship, or the death of a loved one all have a major impact on levels of unhappiness. Surveys show that soon after a divorce, people experience extended periods of unhappiness, often characterized by depression and confusion. These are the situations in which human beings generally have the hardest time becoming happy again. The loss is so large that reference levels need a lot of time to adjust. Shortcuts such as going to a psychiatrist may make us understand and cope with the situation better but will not shorten this necessary phase. Eventually, expectations will adapt to the new level of cumulative reality, but it will take more time than for noncumulative goods.

You may be tempted to try to avoid such large losses by never engaging in cumulative activities that have a risk of being lost. But, as the saying goes, "It's better to have loved and lost than never to have loved at all."

GOALS

In his studies, the psychologist Jonathan Freedman claimed that people with the ability to set objectives for themselves—both short-term and long-term—are happier.[6] The University of Wisconsin neuroscientist Richard Davidson has found that working hard toward a goal and making progress to the point of expecting a goal to be realized don't just activate positive feelings—they also suppress negative emotions such as fear and depression.

According to Michael Argyle, simply having a long-term plan or goal gives people a sense of meaning in life.[7] Progressing toward goals not only gives a purpose to life as a whole but also provides a structure and meaning to daily routines, strengthens social relationships, and helps us weather hard times. The researchers Ian McGregor and

Brian Little proved that point by asking 327 people to rate their personal projects.[8] Projects that were not too difficult or stressful, as well as those leading to positive outcomes and control, all generated happiness. It is important to note that there ought not to be a big gap between the goal and the ability to achieve the goal, because a large gap would lead to individuals feeling disconnected. In other words, goals must be realistic.

Purpose in life can be achieved by committing to goals that are realistic and for which there are resources.

The British philosopher Bertrand Russell espoused the view that the secret to happiness was a formula of enterprise, exploration of one's interests, and the overcoming of obstacles.

Engagement is a particular state of moment-happiness that occurs when we are involved in an activity that (1) is geared toward a goal, (2) is neither too easy nor too difficult, and (3) allows us to obtain frequent feedback from the progress we are making. This is the state of mind that Mihali Csíkszentmihályi labeled "flow." In our view, flow or engagement works because it is a cumulative good, as it is the feeling that a (1) bucket is being filled, (2) the speed of accumulation is just right, and (3) the frequent feedback triggers a positive emotion of progress and accumulation.

Pursuing short- and long-term goals is an assured way to sustain happiness. Two observations are important. The first is that as reality accumulates, the gap between accumulated reality and adaptive references produces a nice flow of happiness. The second observation is that once the goal is accomplished, then the accumulation stops and happiness decays to zero. It is the act of working toward the goal that yields happiness in the first place. Our model supports the view of Ursula Le Guin: "It is good to have an end to journey toward; but it is the journey that matters in the end."

If climbers settle on a goal such as climbing to the summit of Mt. Everest, for instance, they must make huge preparations, beginning with grueling physical training, acquiring the necessary supplies, mapping climbing routes, and arranging travel logistics. It may take months or years finally to get to the base of the mountain and start climbing. The trek to the top is fraught with physical and mental challenges. Danger is ever-present. Climbers are cognizant that many have perished in such a pursuit. Finally, they reach the summit with great excitement, for now they are literally on top of the world. But the euphoria lasts only a few moments before they must begin their descent. Most of the happiness that they will experience won't be derived from summiting the mountain and after, but rather from the hard work it took to get there, the feeling that these efforts will be stored in achieving the goal. Of course, they will experience some more happiness from reflecting on the experience afterward, but not nearly as much as they experienced while progressing toward the goal.

> When I buy that new Mercedes,
> when I put my last kid through college,
> when I pay off the mortgage,
> when I get a promotion,
> when I reach the age of retirement,
> I shall live happily ever after.
>
> Sooner or later we must realize there is no station.
> No one place to arrive at once and for all.
> The true joy of life is in the trip.
> The station is only a dream.
> It constantly outdistances us.
> —From "The Station" by Robert Hastings

Goals are often associated with learning activities, such as music, gardening, wine, and sports. The experience of them is enjoyable in itself, and, as cumulative activities, what we learn stays with us. We may enjoy them even more next time.

According to Michael Argyle, leisure activities that lead to skill building are a crucial source of happiness because they build up a store of knowledge.[9] For instance, practicing a musical instrument can lead to a great deal of happiness. The discipline and skill development required to play an instrument provide the elements for a feeling of accumulation and growth.

Learning to play a musical instrument is accessible and rewarding. Because music is a universal language, people of different abilities, ages, cultures, and nationalities can play together, collaborating in the effort of music making. Music, whether experienced through listening or playing, lends an aesthetic dimension to our lives. The psychologist Erna Barschak, in her study of happiness and unhappiness in girls in different cultures, found that music was mentioned frequently by girls as a source of well-being.[10] Not surprising, people on average listen to music for more than an hour per day.

The importance of music is also illustrated in the adventures of Odysseus, who after the Trojan War wandered for ten years before he saw his home. During his absence, several suitors tried to woo his wife, Penelope. Upon his return, he killed them one by one, with only one exception. He spared the life of a bard, as he could not kill a man who sang so divinely.

Most sports are learning activities, especially if we have a way to keep track of our performance and monitor our progress. All serious golf players have a handicap, a number that measures their skill (the lower the handicap, the better the player). The handicap is essentially a cumulative average of past performance. It is both a way to put players on an equal footing and a score that records a player's past performance.

RELATIONSHIPS

Relationships have many cumulative components. When we get to know our friends and significant others, we fill a bucket of love and trust. Indeed, friendships need to be maintained, cared for, and nurtured; if we don't call, visit, or make an effort, friends fade from our lives. Every time you and your friend go on a trip together, attend a birthday party, or simply meet for a quick cup of coffee adds to your friendship, which continues to strengthen.

The sociologist Norval Glenn claims that married people are consistently far happier that those who never tied the knot or were divorced, separated, or widowed.[11] In our view, a stable relationship such as marriage has features of a cumulative good. In addition to providing emotional help and support to each partner, stable relationships allow partners to accumulate knowledge, memories, trust, and love.

Trust

Trust is a cumulative good: it affects your self-esteem and gives you a sense of security. A clear example of trust is that between a parent and child. Standing on the edge of a swimming pool, the child hesitates a bit when the father or mother asks the child to jump, and then jumps into the pool. The child is unlikely to jump when a stranger asks. The trust between the child and parent has been nurtured over time. During numerous occasions in the past, the child has counted on the parent for protection. In a variety of personal and business circumstances, trust is important to a smooth working relationship and the presence of trust brings assurance and mental peace.

Psyche was a young and beautiful woman whom all men admired and worshipped, but no one would marry her. Aphrodite became jealous of her and asked her son Eros to make Psyche fall in love with the ugliest man on Earth. In an unexpected turn of events, Eros, on seeing Psyche's beauty, fell deeply in love with her. Eros made himself invisible to Psyche and married her so his mother would not find out. They slept together every night and Psyche fell in love with him even though she could not see him. Psyche's two sisters were jealous of her good life and manipulated Psyche into using a lamp to reveal the identity of her husband, Eros, while he slept. However, a drop of hot oil fell on Eros and he was awakened. Angered that she had violated his trust, Eros fled, leaving Psyche to roam the Earth searching for her lover. Luckily, this story happens to have a happy ending, as Zeus took pity and reunited them. The story demonstrates that love cannot flourish once trust is broken: Psyche paid a big price and went through miserable ordeals because she violated Eros's trust.

Here is an example on how trust can be broken. You and your friend will pick red or black independently. If you trust each other and both pick black, then each of you will receive $50. However, if one of you trusts the other and picks black, whereas the other defects and picks red, then the red gets $75 and the black gets $0. If you distrust each other and both pick red, then each of you will receive $10.

What do you expect to happen if this game is played between strangers? Each will find that playing red is better, regardless of what the other does. You win $75 instead of $50 if the other picks black, and you win $10 instead of $0 if the other picks red. The other thinks the same way, and both of you pick red and end up getting $10, instead of the $50 you could have gotten had you trusted each other. This game is a version of the prisoner's dilemma.[12]

Now suppose the players are you and a friend. This means that you will play the game again and again, as you will have recurrent situations involving mutual trust. If you both kept picking black, then you would keep on making $50 each period. Which color would you pick? Most people, probably including you, indeed pick black.

Suppose your friend picks red one of the times. You would get nothing that time and your friend would get $75. What would you do next time? You may be kindhearted and pick black again. Alternatively, you may use tit-for-tat logic and pick red. There is no right answer for an individual player. On average, though, using the tit-for-tat strategy—pick black (cooperate) until your friend picks red (defects) and then pick red in the next period—works quite well. So the idea is that you do trust your friend as long as your trust is reciprocated, but if your friend breaks that trust, then you retaliate in proportion to the offense but not more. This achieves the recovery of mutual trust and deters your friend from breaking the trust.

In this situation and in many real-life situations (marriage, business partnership, sports teams), trust improves happiness for all. But unhappiness is caused if trust is broken. Trust is a cumulative good that has the potential for high payoffs and thus needs to be cultivated. We see the importance of trust in everyday life. We trust our neighbor to drop our child off at school if we are sick. We seek advice from those whom we trust. To sustain love, we need trust. Though trust is not an emotion, it does influence the happiness seismogram. If Jane trusts Beth to babysit her child, then this means she feels that her child will be safe. Without trust, Jane would be anxious and stressed the entire time she is away from her child. Thus, Jane's happiness seismogram will be higher in the "trust" scenario and lower in the "lack of trust" scenario.

Resentment and Forgiveness

In the same way that we have basic goods and basic bads, we also have cumulative goods and cumulative bads. Accumulating bad things and bad memories is an impediment to happiness. One incident of bad karma is bad enough, but an accumulating series of incidents produces a steady flow of unhappiness.

In relationships, negative accumulation produces resentment. Studies show that a good predictor of divorce is when one of the spouses sees the other's defect as permanent, as opposed to transient.[13] Hence, every negative event accumulates because "he is like this," or "she has always been like that." In contrast, harmonious couples see the defect of the other as transient. "Today we had a heated discussion, which is unusual. We are fine"; in contrast to: "This is the eleventh time that you have done this." Blacklisting your significant other—or, for that matter, any other person—is a way to accumulate negativity and is a sure recipe for unhappiness.

Unfortunately, resentment can go on for centuries. There is the story of a Spanish general, known as the "Great Captain," who in 1503 defeated the French in Italian territories. Three hundred years later, Napoleon ordered his tomb in Granada destroyed. When one of us visited what remains of the Great General's tomb, the person in charge of cleaning the church commented, "Resentment, this is the nature of the human heart."

What is the point of thinking back on those stupid discussions you once had with your partner? Our happiness recipe suggests you should just let it go. Hence, our recommendation is to accumulate the good moments and perceive the bad moments as transient, in other words, keep beautiful photographs of those holidays when you went to the coast but trash those e-mails in which you argued for days. Forgiveness is the way to let go of accumulated bads.

Forgiveness, and attributing offences to passing causes, is a way to neutralize the buildup of negative emotions. We will be unhappy for a while, but the negative feelings will dissipate if we let the law of adaptation follow its course.

In John Milton's *Paradise Lost*, Adam and Eve face the fundamental challenge of any romantic relationship—the balance between autonomy and interdependence.[14] A marital dispute between them (in Book 9) leads to an escalation of misunderstandings and their eventual physical separation. Eve, now alone, is tempted by Satan embodied in the serpent to eat the forbidden fruit, with dire results. Modern-day couples are no different, as relationships are destroyed by exacerbating slight disagreements into great divides. Milton beautifully illustrates the power of repentance and forgiveness that unites Eve with Adam. "Forsake me not thus, Adam" (in Book 10) is Eve's moving lament that is felt by Adam. "Soon his heart relented" and he moved toward reconciliation, declaring, "Let us no more contend, nor blame."

For Catholics, the practice of confession helps to alleviate the impact of one's sins and guilt. We are not arguing that you should ask for forgiveness as a gimmick—the priest might let you off the hook, but your spouse will definitely have his or her limit. There should be a sincerity and genuine desire to modify behavior for forgiveness to diminish your negativity.

Storing Memories in a Bucket

An amnesic individual receives an electric shock from a faulty toaster. The next day he attempts to use the same toaster again. Clearly, his experience with the toaster was painful, but he does not recall the pain.

Our memories may not be as faulty as that of an amnesiac, but we do store only some experiences—pleasurable and painful—in our memories. The memories of pleasurable experiences provide a source of joy and happiness and therefore improve our long-term happiness. Conversely, the memories of painful experiences such as a divorce or an accident can be a source of unhappiness.

Recognizing that memories are a cumulative good that is stored in a bucket is the first step in choosing how we treat events in life. For example, if someone cuts us off while driving, do we want to engage in road rage? It is not just the negative emotion of the moment that a tit-for-tat reaction causes, but such a negative experience will be stored in our memory bucket. So just relax and let the hurried driver pass you by.

But life will offer us a myriad of pleasurable and painful experiences. Our smart choices could increase the frequency of positive experiences and reduce the frequency of negative experiences. Nevertheless, the bucket of memories will contain both the joyful and sad times.

Memories are cumulative goods (or bads) and to some degree we have control over which memories to draw on as we live our lives. Some people have a remarkable ability to draw from the positive experiences even when they have lived hard lives. Others on the other hand, dwell on a few negative experiences though they have lived largely prosperous and comfortable lives. A telltale sign of a happy person is the ability to use the memory bucket wisely—by recalling easily past positive experiences and letting negative experiences fade.

HAPPINESS IN ACTION

Select one hobby or interest and focus on developing it over time. It could be anything from gardening and athletics to reading and spiritual practice. Keep a diary to track your progress, and take time as you go to appreciate how much you've progressed.

CHAPTER 11

Reframing

The last of the human freedoms is to choose one's attitudes.
—Viktor Frankl

Imagine you are stuck in traffic. No one is moving, and as you look out the window you see several agitated drivers. There is an accident ahead and it will take some time to clear the way. You feel tension building in your muscles and clouding your mind, but instead you imagine that you are sitting on a giant ball about eight thousand miles of diameter that is spinning at about sixty-seven thousand miles per hour. You realize you are on an awesome Disneyland ride and a smile breaks out on your face.

That is reframing.

Of course, the fact is that you are still stuck in the traffic. As soon as you forget about your wild ride through space, you're right back in the car and you lapse back into frustration. Finally, the traffic clears and you are moving again. A sense of relief takes over and your mind drifts to the chores you need to do before the day is over.

Are we as happy as we could be? The truth—and the good news—is that most of us could do better. To do that we need to take control of the rudder and start being in charge of our own well-being; so let's explore how we can train our minds to see the glass being half-full more often.

Trapped in a Nazi concentration camp during World War II, Viktor Frankl set for himself the goal of simply surviving.[1] His parents and family members died in one of the camps, but he survived. Based on his experiences helping himself and other prisoners survive in the concentration camp, Frankl wrote his influential book *Man's Search for Meaning*. In his view, humanity's primary motivational force is to search for meaning in life and to work toward achieving it. He insists that meaning can be found even in the most hopeless situations.

CHOOSING TO BE HAPPY

We have argued that most emotions are triggered by comparisons between a reality and some expectation. Expectations themselves change over time, however. Recall the equation:

HAPPINESS *equals*
REALITY *minus* SHIFTING EXPECTATIONS

The obvious way to be happier is to improve reality. We have said a great deal about it; for each type of good or activity, we want to keep an eye on how expectations change over time. Adaptive goods produce happiness only if they are consumed at an increasing rate, and conspicuous goods require us to be "in the right pond." Basic goods and activities, as well as goods and activities that accumulate, provide a stream of happiness.

We will now show a third type of activity that, like basic and cumulative goods, produces assured happiness. We call these reframing activities. Reframing activities are all those purposeful activities that make us see reality in a different way, reset our expectations, or create new comparisons.

Extracting more happiness from the same reality is a skill that can be learned, and perhaps it is one of the golden keys to well-being in life. We have a limited amount of money and time to spend on different goods and activities to obtain a nice flow of happydons over time. To this end, the game plan is to divide our resources between two fronts. The first is to improve reality by buying and doing things. The second is to spend time in improving how our mind encodes and processes this reality to create happiness.

How much potential for happiness is there in changing attitudes and expectations? Studies of happiness across individuals converge to the 15/35/50 rule. Life circumstances—in which country or region of the world you live, what kind of community is around you, what your income and employment status are, whether you were raised in a house with divorced parents or you were an adopted child—are responsible for about 15 percent of your satisfaction with life.

Intentional behaviors—what you purposefully do yourself to become a happier person—explain 35 percent of the variability in happiness across individuals.

Studies done with identical twins suggest that genetic factors do influence happiness. According to these studies, genes explain up to 50 percent of the variation in happiness levels across individuals. So, a big part of how happy you are depends on how happy your parents were and their parents before them.[2]

If we just focus on the 15/35 on which we can act, we see that changing our attitudes may be *more than twice* as effective as trying to change external circumstances.

MULTIPLE REPRESENTATIONS OF REALITY

The mind is its own place, and in itself
Can make a Heav'n of Hell; a Hell of Heav'n
—John Milton, *Paradise Lost*

On November 23, 1951, there was a well-contested, but rough, football game between Dartmouth and Princeton. The game resulted in a broken nose for a Princeton player and a broken leg for a Dartmouth player. The psychologists Albert Hastorf and Hadley Cantril asked a group of students at each school to watch a film of the game and to take note of any infractions they observed. All of the students watched the same game and used the same rules for recording violations, but the two groups saw the game very differently. The Princeton students recorded an average of 9.8 violations committed by Dartmouth, but the Dartmouth students saw an average of only 4.3 violations committed by their team. The researchers concluded that while these students were watching the same game, they were actually *seeing* different games. They remarked: "The 'thing' is not the same for different people whether the 'thing' is a football game, a presidential candidate, communism, or spinach."[3]

Similarly, let's examine two colleagues who both took their first jobs and spent the first two years of their careers in the small town of West Lafayette, Indiana. One fondly recalls the experience of living and working in West Lafayette, but the other was only too glad to finally move away. The one who enjoyed living there found it to be a place with affordable living, friendly neighbors, short commutes, and low crime. The other, who was unhappy, saw it as a place with cold winters, a small airport, and limited choices of restaurants and entertainment. Now these two people may have had genuinely different preferences and weighed the varied dimensions of the town and job differently, but within limits, people do have a choice as to how they see the world—half full or half empty. People who focus on positive dimensions and deemphasize negative ones are going to experience more positive emotions and consequently be happier than those for whom nothing is ever good enough.

In a physical sense, the visual impact of the same river, landscape, or mountain changes with perspective. Similarly, our mind's perspective makes us see the same reality in a brighter or a darker sense. The role of the fool in Shakespeare's plays was to make us see that many of the world's pursuits are ridiculous. The fool is naturally wise and perceives simple but profound truths that we often deny.

A dose of humor and gratitude can be the remedy to extract greater happiness from the same reality: saying an honest "Good morning" to the barista who makes your coffee won't just make her smile; it will make you happier, too.

CONQUEST OF ADAPTATION

Let's explore some ways to influence expectation so that our lives can be happier within the same reality.

Manage Expectations

In their research on how expectations change, Allan Chen and Akshay Rao found that people are happier after experiencing a false alarm because their expectations went down, and the same outcome is perceived as a gain.[4]

Suppose you lost the new sunglasses you bought two weeks ago. They were cool and also quite expensive. A few hours later you found the sunglasses in your jacket. The relief of finding your glasses is so great that it may compensate for the previous anxiety.

Be smart about how you adjust your expectations. If your friends tell you about an excellent movie, go ahead and buy the tickets. As you wait in the theater lobby, you can either get completely psyched to see the movie or you can moderate your expectations. You may want to read what the critics have to say about the movie, since their very nature is to find fault and exaggerate minor blemishes. If you control your exuberance regarding the movie and expect little, then it is more likely that you will enjoy the surprise that the movie is in fact quite good and much better than the critics had opined.

Contrast Reality Favorably

The psychologists Tversky and Griffin argue that a positive life experience such as a romantic interlude adds to the endowment of the bucket of happy memories, but it also makes the subsequent similar experiences less exciting through contrast.[5] The key to happiness then lies in recalling joyful events, but comparing present events to less desirable past events. In some cases, the comparison of a present experience to a past experience may be automatic. But often, we do have freedom in choosing the past experience with which to contrast the present event. One simple trick is to go ahead and start talking to your friends about how delicious the pizza you are having now is compared to the one you often have at your local pizza parlor. Our advice is to store your fabulous experiences—such as watching the World Cup with friends—in your bucket of happy memories to be recalled fondly in the future. But extract the most joy out of a current experience by comparing it to a less favorable event of the past.

Transform Adaptive Goods into Cumulative Goods

We know that cumulative goods can be a source of happiness, but certain goods are clearly not cumulative and others clearly are. Some goods fall into a gray area, however, and it is up to us to choose how we allow them to be viewed in our minds as one type or the other.

What is our recommendation? The best mind-set is to be able to use both frames of mind. For Felipe, the researcher, the three-compared-to-two publications per year mind-set is useful for maintaining research drive and motivation, whereas the fourteen-compared-to-twelve total papers mind-set is useful for being happy and avoiding being too hard on himself. Being able to use multiple frames helps us see reality in a rich way.

The painter Joan Miró wrote, "As you see, I work very slowly. As I work on a canvas, I fall in love with it, love that is born of slow understanding. Slow understanding of nuances—concentrated—which the sun gives. Joy of learning to understand a tiny blade of grass in a landscape. Why belittle it? A blade of grass is as enchanting as a tree or a mountain. Apart from the primitives and the Japanese, almost everyone overlooks this which is so divine."[6]

The father of one of the authors likes the simple outdoor activities of hiking and mushroom hunting. He enjoys going mushroom hunting on every trip he takes, as if it were the first time. He does not let satiation and adaptation reduce his joy. In fact, for him, mushroom hunting is a refreshing activity full of novelty and learning. He likes to learn where the mushrooms have grown this season, and likes to show off the new mushroom sites he has discovered. In this context, the activity of mushroom hunting is an experience with cumulative aspects as well as healthy social comparison elements that all contribute to enjoyment. We can all find something that we love to do and for which our joy remains undiminished. It could be attending poetry classes, cooking, painting, or dancing.

Hobbies such as gardening or caring for an orchard are peaceful, lasting, and rewarding. These activities provide plenty of novelty, and can easily be seen as cumulative, as things always change and grow.

Broader Comparisons

Have you seen the "India driving" or "Bangalore traffic" videos on YouTube? Instead of complaining that traffic lights are always red, think how dreadful it would be to live in cities without any traffic lights at all. Alternatively, take a minute to be satisfied with the fact that you can communicate so fast with your friends living in Australia now—something your grandparents could not have even imagined.

How often do we complain about the government, its bureaucracy and corruption? We take democracy or the relatively civilized way in which modern cities operate for granted. We fail to appreciate that a few generations ago, or in some countries even today, people live in constant fear of wars, threats, and the tyranny of some autocrat.

Detachment

We experience great unhappiness when something we own is lost or damaged: forgetting our wallet at a restaurant, discovering that someone scratched our new car or that someone stole our motorcycle. But we are necessarily bound to experience many such unavoidable losses in our lifetime. Is there some shield to protect us from the resulting unhappiness?

In fact, there is, and that is by cultivating an attitude of detachment. The opposite of detachment is attachment. Attachment is the mechanism by which our expectations adapt to what we have. Once we buy an object, now it is ours and we do not want to lose it!

Have you ever observed that some people suffer when they buy a new car? They are anxious not to get a single scratch—even to the point of not using the car! One of our colleagues always parked his fancy new car in the last spot so that he wouldn't be sandwiched by two other cars. This was his way of reducing the probability of getting his car scratched by someone else's door or someone crashing into it. Before purchasing the car, he did not anticipate that his shift in expectation would actually enslave him in this way.

Here is a sound strategy for emotional regulation: if someone dings your car, instead of becoming upset, realize that you no longer have to worry about your car being in perfect condition upon your return every time you park in a public space.

The practice of detachment, treating things that we use as if they were on loan, is mentally very healthy. This mitigates adaptation, and avoids the anxiety of a possible or actual loss.

Epicurus argued that when eating, one should not eat too richly, for it could lead to dissatisfaction later, such as the grim realization that one could not afford such delicacies in the future.

Karma yoga, mostly practiced within the Hindu religion, has detachment as one of its core practices. The key idea is that you should act in accordance with your duty and without being attached to the fruits of your deeds. Many scientific discoveries have been made because the scientist pursued his curiosity and passion without any consideration of reward. The practice of detachment is the cornerstone of some historically influential spiritual philosophies such as those of the Buddhists and Franciscans.

Bad Things Happen

Life is not a bed of roses, as the saying goes. Bad things do happen. Our loved ones fall ill; we lose jobs, or get divorced. How can we make such events more bearable? We are not Buddhist monks who, through extensive training in detachment, have learned to regulate negative emotions. In modern times, most people have faith in God, but do not see every disaster as a curse from God. In Greek mythology, bad things were believed to happen as a result of curses from the gods. The House of Atreus had a curse that went on for generations. Agamemnon, who led the Greeks against Troy, and his brother Menelaus were descendents of this family. The Trojan War was fought because of the abduction of Helen of Troy who was the wife of Menelaus. Agamemnon was killed by his wife's lover. The cause of all the misfortunes of this house was a wicked deed of an ancestor, a king of Lydia, Tantalus. The curse eventually ended after several generations.

We are not likely to blame our misfortunes on an ancestor or our own deeds from previous lives. Such beliefs persist in some cultures, but are probably not held strongly in the West today. People who have internalized the concept of karma are more accepting of bad fortune, figuring it is the inevitable consequence of bad deeds of a family member or their previous lives.

When a misfortune or tragedy befalls us, we ask, "Why me?" In his powerful book *When Bad Things Happen to Good People,* Harold Kushner argues that some things happen for no reason and are purely random. In such unfortunate situations—losing a loved one, contracting a serious disease, or becoming disabled because of an accident—a constructive approach is to ask what I should do next to take charge of the life I have now.

Fortunately, there are ways of reframing that help us deal with negative events. Suppose you have hurt your elbow to the extent that you will be unable to play tennis in the near future. You love playing tennis and are deeply disappointed. One way to mitigate this loss is for you to develop interests in less demanding sports such as hiking, or take up a card game such as bridge or poker. This is an active form of adaptation, which will reduce the impact of your bad elbow on your joyful activities. You will miss playing tennis for a while, but the negative effects of not being able to play tennis will last longer if you do not pick up other engaging activities as a substitute.

There is no adaptation to chronic pain or mental anguish. Medicines are the best source to alleviate such suffering. Reframing could help a little, but its effectiveness has a limit.

Cancer patients are often able to come to grips with their situation and are able to lift their spirits if they are not in pain. They begin to see a broader meaning in life and tune in intimately to the inevitable life and death process of all existence. To most of us who are not facing the certainty of death within a definite time period, death happens only to others.

For people who have sufficient income for food, shelter, and clothing and are in good enough health to enjoy a soft breeze and the warmth of the sun's rays, a proper mental perspective goes a long way in deriving more joy from the same reality. The conquest of adaptation is not dictated by our genes. We are all capable of experiencing joy from "dew drops on the ear of the corn" if we choose to change our perspective.

The Anxiety of Choice

Suppose you're shopping for a new laptop online. As you surf Web sites, you encounter hundreds of models, brands, and styles of computers. Eventually you shortlist the ones you prefer, and once you have about four or five to choose from, that's when it gets hard. Therefore, you end up picking one of them but letting go of the other four. At this point, the key is simply to forget about the others and the advantages they would bring you and focus on the one you chose and how great it is.

Too many options create what we call "choice overload." Too many choices require performing too many comparisons. Shops that have a lot of variety increase the number of customers who enter the store, but lower the number of purchases. In a well-known study, when people are offered a few flavors of jam, they end up purchasing something. When they are offered many flavors, however, they tend simply to walk away without buying anything.[7]

Gerd Gigerenzer, the head of the ABC research group in Berlin, argues that some simple decision rules work very well in real-life situations. They help us to avoid the anxiety of choice, as well as produce decent choices. For example, one such rule is elimination by aspects. To see how this rule works, first rank the criteria from most important to least important. For example, to choose among applicants for a job, suppose the criteria, sorted by importance, are: work experience, education level, and people skills. Elimination by aspects would take all candidates and eliminate those who are poor on the first criterion. In this case, all the candidates with no work experience would be eliminated. For the remaining candidates, we move to the second criterion and, again, eliminate the ones who do not have a college degree.

We proceed this way until we are left with one sufficiently good candidate or there is a tie among a few candidates. How do we choose among these? We often make a simple, but powerful, recommendation to our students: when facing a situation in which you have to choose between two or more alternatives of roughly equal value, it is completely rational to . . . choose at random! It turns out that this simple rule of elimination by aspects chooses the best alternative quite often.[8]

The legendary basketball coach John Wooden used to say: "Never look back."[9] Comparisons with what we could have chosen are bound to make us, more often than not, unhappy. In these comparisons, half the time we win, but half the time we lose. As losses count double, we have a net loss of happiness, which could easily be avoided. Research done by Dan Ariely shows that closing doors increases happiness, as one concentrates resources on making the best of what we have chosen.[10] It is like this for couples who get married and promise to be faithful for the rest of their lives—forswearing all other men and women on the planet.

This is simply because human beings naturally tend to adapt to what life provides them once they cannot see a way of changing it. Daniel Gilbert, a professor of psychology at Harvard University, has been studying the topic for many years and he believes that we have a psychological immune system that lets us feel enduring happiness, even when things are not going our way.

Closing doors may be tough when the decision is being made, but once decided, it is a great strategy for happiness. In other words, move on!

Optimism

It has been found that people who are optimistic, who think that the best of all futures will occur, tend to be happier. In our framework, they obtain lots of happydons from anticipation of good events. When the future is not as good as predicted, they ignore the moment and jump into dreaming about the next future. Optimists attribute bad fortune to passing causes and good fortune to permanent causes, such as their abilities. Clearly, such an extreme form of optimism requires a certain amount of self-deception. Is self-deception a good recipe for happiness? Rationally speaking, the negative side of self-deception is that it leads to poor decision making, because the model of the world that we hold in our mind is not correct. For instance, we may fail to take protective measures in anticipation of bad outcomes that might occur.

But being too realistic may not be a good formula for happiness! What is the point of always being too worried about the future? Bestsellers such as *The Power of Now* by Eckhart Tolle are very explicit about creating happiness in the mind by finding awareness of a deep inner self that is unaffected by external circumstance.[11] This and other spiritual practices take time.

. We need to be aware, however, that a dose of optimism is good for increasing happiness but not for sound decision making. When it comes to decision making, the more realistic we become about the functioning of the world, the better. Nonetheless, as we are not making decisions all the time, why not spend time and effort in constructing a happy mind refuge that we need to abandon only when making hard decisions?

Emotional Regulation

Thich Nhat Hanh is a world expert in the study of anger.[12] He suggests mindful meditation to control anger. For instance, when it comes to anger management, what is best: to burst or to contain? Shall we let ourselves be carried away by anger, so that anger goes away? Or shall we contain the anger? Which of the two strategies is more effective in reducing the likelihood of future anger outbursts? Research shows that the first strategy has a flaw. These anger outbursts, which might alleviate anger in the short run, make us more prone to become angry in the future, as attacks of anger become a habit. In contrast, holding back anger turns out to be smarter. For one thing, anger dissipates sooner than expected. More important, we become less prone to become angry in the future. Incidents of anger may be fun to watch in reality shows, but the fact is that anger destroys marriages, family life, and friendships, and poisons community and international relations.

Again, incorporating strategies for daily emotional regulation can indeed increase happiness. The study of strategies for emotional regulation is part of the field of study called positive psychology. Martin Seligman of the University of Pennsylvania pioneered this area of research.[13] Nowadays, there are more than two hundred university courses on positive psychology across the United States. The basic idea behind the new approach is very similar to what Buddhist monks have been doing for hundreds of years: training their minds to be happier. Happiness is like a butterfly: it cannot be directly sought; we must do other things for happiness to arise as a consequence.

CONQUEST OF SOCIAL COMPARISON

An Abu Dhabi businessperson paid $9 million for the license plate number "5." His cousin, also a business man, paid $14 million for the number "1."

People who buy such outrageously priced items (such as $11,000 jeans and a $300,000 cell phone) are seeking prestige and to satisfy their desire to belong to an elite group. Shakespeare said *cucullus non facit monachum* ("the cowl does not make the monk"). Yet some rich people are unhappy as they compare themselves to people who are even richer than they are.

Even gods are not exempt from social comparison. In Greek mythology, Aphrodite (Venus in Latin) was the goddess of love and beauty, but she unleashed her fury on a mere mortal, Psyche, because she could not stand the fame of Psyche's beauty.

If you are reading this book, then we can safely venture that you live in a society that has many conveniences that would have been hard for our ancestors to imagine. Unfortunately, the knowledge of what is possible has also greatly increased. The lifestyles of the rich and famous are paraded daily in your living room through TV, movies, and the Internet. The desire for social comparison and competition is built into the fast flow of information and advertisements and it has heightened your awareness of how green the grass can be on the other side.

In remote villages of India, people are quite poor. They barely have enough food to survive, their homes are made of simple materials, and they lack sanitation and electricity. Nevertheless, these families strive to outdo each other at weddings. They spend their life savings for weddings and consider it a matter of shame if proper food and jewelry are not offered. The government of India forbids dowry and limits the money spent on feasts, but the custom often trumps the law.

The objects of social comparison are moving targets. If you move to a more prosperous neighborhood, you begin to compare yourself to the new neighbors and comparisons with less affluent neighbors of the past fade. The lesson, once again, is that improving your reality will not increase happiness if expectations increase as well.

Monks in a monastery become absorbed in their daily routines and the rituals of the house and are less likely to compare themselves to other monks on material dimensions, but they may actually feel competitive on their knowledge of scriptures and the purity of their religious practices. Most of us do not live in such homogenous environments with uniform expectations. We have a myriad of options for hobbies and entertainment, which make our lives colorful and enhance our pleasure. We should enjoy the roses we grow. However, our joy is diminished as soon as we begin to compare our roses to our neighbor's roses. Some people become obsessed with making these comparisons, and the joy derived from every object is tempered by envy of something that someone else possesses.

Happy people count their blessings and are thankful for what they have. All of us have the capacity to define our life and find meaning and purpose in a way that gives us joy and makes us feel good. Dimensions of comparison include material possessions, family life, friendship, hobbies, public service, and religion. Adam Smith said, perhaps with a bit of exaggeration, that "In ease of body and peace of mind, all the different ranks of life are nearly upon a level, and the beggar, who suns himself by the side of the highway, possesses that security which kings are fighting for."

A person of modest means may possess fewer material objects, but he can enjoy his family life, friendship, and interest in gardening so long as he focuses on the goodness of his own life. He has fewer burdens in having to manage his wealth and he doesn't need to wonder if his friends like him because of his financial success or expect him to share his wealth.

We should learn to enjoy things solely for what they are and not for how good they are in comparison to what others have. In some jobs such as practicing medicine or teaching, it is easier to see one's contributions on dimensions other than wealth acquisition. Even though there are plenty of dissatisfied doctors and teachers (because they see life in terms of comparisons), they do have the choice to define their work as reducing suffering and developing young minds. In some professions, however, money has become the yardstick of success. Our lives have multiple dimensions and even if we focus on numerous measures of success at work, we can choose to see broader meaning in our lives.

Some people take great joy in seeing that their children get a good education and become responsible adults. Others are active in their church group and receive friendship and spiritual fulfillment from their circle. Still others are avid readers, or enjoy hiking or fly-fishing. Some people like to cook and enjoy getting together with their friends for hearty meals. Some people like to garden and find relaxation in growing vegetables and flowers. We can emphasize the activities in our lives that give us joy and take our minds off negative emotions. Thus, this first step toward conquering social comparison is to begin to see the fullness of life on multiple dimensions. Let us not be seduced by advertisements shouting that happiness is attainable only though some unreachable standard of wealth, status, or beauty.

Ancient wisdom and modern research show that happiness cannot be attained by wealth and fame.

King Solomon, seeking happiness in the pursuit of pleasure, concluded, "All is vanity and vexation of spirit." The Bible records in the second chapter of Ecclesiastes, "I wanted to find out what was best for us during the short time we have on this earth. So I decided to make myself happy with wine. . . . I built houses and planted vineyards. . . . I owned slaves. . . . I had more sheep and goats than anyone. . . . Foreign rulers brought me silver, gold, and precious treasures. Men and women sang for me, and I had many wives who gave me great pleasure, I was the most famous person who ever lived in Jerusalem." Solomon summed up the pleasure derived from his fame and fortune as "simply chasing the wind."

Modern research suggests that happiness does increase with wealth, but the increase is minor beyond a certain level of income. King Solomon was already at a very high level of prosperity and no wonder he failed to obtain additional pleasure from all his worldly pursuits. His disappointment seems to have arisen from attaining all his desires so easily. Fortunately, most of us are not in Solomon's position. We have needs and wants that we can strive to fulfill. Happiness comes to us in achieving these wants. Working toward a higher level of job satisfaction, harmonious family life, and good relations with neighbors and friends boosts happiness. If a genie instantly gave us everything we desire—wealth, fame, and love—then we would have all we want but remain unfulfilled.

Happiness is in making an effort to fill the glass little by little, not in inheriting a full glass. In the United States, there are coaches for very wealthy children who teach them to appreciate the good fortune that is handed to them. Rich people are unhappy because they engage in excessive social comparison. Adam Smith noted, "With the greater part of rich people, the chief enjoyment of riches, which in their eyes is never as complete as when they appear to possess those decisive masses of opulence which nobody can possess but themselves." No wonder owning the number "1" for a license plate becomes so high a priority in life for some folks!

CONQUEST OF SATIATION

There are two great neutralizers of satiation. The first one is variety or novelty: repetition dulls our senses and makes things seem routine. After enjoying a day at the museum, it is not a good idea to go back to the same museum the next day. Go to a sports event or watch a movie. The second neutralizer of satiation is time. If you wait a while to go back to the museum, then the experience will be fresh and rewarding. Of course, using our fundamental equation, adjusted for satiation, we could compute the optimal time interval between consumption for each and every possible activity. But just use your instincts. Do not buy a five-day museum pass to save a little money. You will most likely have seen the entire museum after the first day, and by the fifth day you will be sitting on a bench in the courtyard of the museum wishing you were someplace else.

Many books give advice on how to reinvigorate relationships. The principle is simple: do not allow experiences to become routine and dull. The *Kama Sutra* is an ancient Indian manual on the art of lovemaking. It was written by Vatsyayana when he was leading the life of a religious student at Benares (now Varanasi—the holiest city in India). The *Kama Sutra* deals with the conduct of joyful life, but part 2 (out of seven parts) of the book, which focuses on sexual unions, is the most well-known. Sex sells! Various ways of embracing, kissing, and sexual positions are described to enhance pleasure. In ancient India, works of art depicted nudity, romantic themes, and sexual unions. The most famous example can be seen at the Khajuraho temple complex in central India. It is a bit strange that in the land where the *Kama Sutra* originated, the depiction of sex and even kissing on television and film is taboo.

Even children like variety and novelty. Repeatedly show them the same toy, and soon they will become indifferent and begin to cry even though their bellies are full and their diapers are dry. When a child cries for no reason except out of boredom or for want of attention, show him a mirror: children like to look at themselves, as their own image is still very much a novelty to them. They do not like to look at a crying face (in this case, their own) and usually stop complaining.

Nevertheless, we should not be hooked on variety and novelty to the degree that we demand more and more excitement and enjoy nothing. Teenagers nowadays have a tremendous variety of entertainment possibilities (television, computer, MP3 player) but they end up not really focusing on anything and get bored quickly.

One way to counteract satiation is to focus on what makes objects and experiences different, rather than on what makes them similar. In some parts of the world and in some seasons, potatoes are one of the few affordable foods. Students who live in dormitories in Pilani, Rajasthan (a desert town) know it well. Some students complain of being served potatoes every day. The others, however, see each preparation of potatoes as distinct and appreciate the meal every day. Potatoes can be served as a soupy vegetable or in a dry form—they could be made spicy, baked, or fried. They have a great variety of potatoes—from tiny balls to large ones. To the group who complains, it is just a potato that is inflicted on them each day and they became satiated long ago. To those who enjoy their meals, each preparation is unique and looks, smells, and tastes different each day. Using reframing, one group has learned to curb their satiation and derives more pleasure from each meal. The complaining group is tired of eating potatoes, as they fail to appreciate the underlying variety in the preparation of meals with potatoes.

Often it happens that when we have a wider and deeper interest in things and life, we appreciate differences more. If we look at objects in a superficial way, then we will need dramatic changes to satisfy us. A single rose goes through an amazing transformation from its bud stage to its full bloom, and we should learn, or maybe just practice more often, the habit of appreciating the shape, color, and smell of the rose throughout its short lifecycle. Dullness and boredom are experienced if we see the roses as just a patch of flowers. Individual roses alter their form each day, but the patch of flowers indeed remains the same.

We have the choice to see each day as a new day full of hope and experiences. We also have the choice of treating each day as a "Groundhog Day," in which we basically re-live the same day over and over.

We all know people who enjoy their meals and relish every bite. They drink and converse with exuberance. Even if their work is toil, their spirits are awakened during the meal. Others see food only as a way to fill their stomachs. They are uninterested in the flavors, colors, and tastes of the food. They are satiated and their senses awaken only occasionally when there is a feast or festival; all the rest is routine. The happiness seismogram for such people will show a low level of moment-happiness.

Although we can't expect that everyone will find joy in every meal, it is helpful for increasing happiness to find joy in something that you do on a recurring basis. You may enjoy reading books, collecting stamps, biking, gardening, playing sports, or meeting people; whichever you choose, you should cultivate some interests. Then enjoy those activities you choose by seeking variety and novelty—add a few dance moves to your life! *Kama Sutra* also recommends that we participate in festivals, social gatherings, drinking parties, picnics, dice games, sporting, and decorating each other.

Bertrand Russell said in *The Conquest of Happiness,* "Think of the different things that may be noticed in the course of a country walk. One man may be interested in the birds, another in the vegetation, another in the geology, another in the agriculture and so on. Any one of these things is interesting if it interests you, and, other things being equal, the man who is interested in any one of them is better adapted to the world than the man who is not interested." The conquest of satiation begins with seeing the world as a giant playground offering new challenges to overcome and new adventures to experience daily.

THE CENTER OF THE UNIVERSE

Narcissus was so beautiful that even the loveliest maidens longed for him. But he was indifferent to all and paid attention to none. One of the girls whose love he scorned prayed to the gods, and they answered her prayer: "May he who loves not others love himself." Then he saw his own reflection in the water and fell in love with it. He was so fixated that he leaned perpetually over the pool until he died of starvation.

We all seem to have, to some degree, a preoccupation with ourselves. When you do not feel like talking in a social gathering, simply ask people about their travels or children. Dale Carnegie's secret to good conversation is to let others talk for themselves—listening is also a good exercise. You can then relax and listen because people love to talk about themselves.

It is commonplace to read about politicians and captains of industry in trouble because they consider themselves above the law. They are so obsessed with their charm, fame, or power that they become self-destructive. Most of us are not as extreme in our obsession with ourselves as the legendary Narcissus or as drunk with power as the mortal Hitler, but we all need to reframe our thoughts to take an interest in others and the world around us.

One way to connect with the world is to consider others as extensions of ourselves. In Hindu and Buddhist philosophies, there is a belief in reincarnation. With such a belief, it does not make sense to be angry with someone, because in some past lifetime the person could have been your own mother, for example. When we reduce our preoccupation with ourselves, we develop admiration for others, which diminishes envy. Consequently, negative emotions are reduced in duration and intensity, and positive emotions are enhanced.

We need to watch our own interests. As the famous Rabbi Hillel said, "If I am not for myself, then who will be for me? And if I am only for myself, then what am I?" Therefore, there is a balance between guarding our own interests and caring for others' well-being. Often there is no conflict between these goals, however. Take Bill Gates as an example; today, as chairman of Microsoft he works for his own financial success, but he also cares deeply about the suffering of people in Africa. Warren Buffett and Richard Branson are great businesspeople as well as great philanthropists.

The total happiness is higher for a person who has compassion and love for others, other things being equal. To develop compassion and love for others, we need to develop a genuine interest in others' well-being. A person who is preoccupied solely with his own well-being cannot have genuine love. Moreover, love is a source of happiness in itself, but it also enhances the happiness realized in other experiences. Playing sports, taking a walk, or watching a sunset all seem more pleasurable when you are in the company of someone you love. You should not feel like the center of the universe; you are one of the seven billion points of light and each is special and sacred.[14]

NARRATING ONE'S LIFE

Life is full of ups and downs. Today you might feel miserable because work was stressful and traffic was backed up for miles, but tomorrow you might go out for a fun dinner with friends and you will experience only joy and contentment. As we have seen in previous chapters, our life seismogram normally exhibits a great variety of positive and negative emotions.

Life is not a rosy paradise, and we lack the control over reality that would enable us to avoid losses. We meet someone who might be "the one," only to be disappointed. We get a parking ticket, sprain an ankle, or catch the flu. Our cars break down, our computers freeze up, and our bikes get stolen. How can the happiness balance possibly end up being positive if losses count twice as much as gains?

One possibility we suggest is to plan for a certain amount of loss. For instance, count on catching the flu once per winter, breaking a bone once every ten years, and provide a budget of some hundreds of dollars for possible parking tickets and property loss. Some of us actually do this! Most people don't, however, and they still manage to be happy. What is it that they do?

The answer is to use life narratives to achieve emotional cancellation. Life narratives are ways to connect negative events with positive events to start making sense of things. As events happen, they are stored in some few accounts, each being a chapter of our life narrative. Positive events increase the account and negative events reduce the account. But it is the net balance in the account that triggers emotions. The goal is to avoid the feelings of loss by connecting negative events with similarly sized positive events. Mathematically, this is exactly the way cumulative goods operate. Some people are better than others at creating these connections and building a coherent life narrative.

Here is an illustrative example. Olivier still remembers his great disappointment when his application to a study abroad program was rejected. He felt as though his whole world was falling apart; he had always wanted to go to Italy to study art history. Instead, he ended up staying at his university for his junior year. But every cloud has a silver lining. The next semester he met Veronica. He found his hands sweaty and his heart pounding just thinking of her. We have all gone through that at some point of our lives—indeed, they fell in love right from the start and it didn't take long until they decided to tie the knot.

After a few years, looking back at some old pictures, Olivier remembered how Italy was his first option and, if he had not been rejected, he would probably not have met the love of his life.

From a purely logical viewpoint, the two events are independent; had he spent that year in Italy, he would have had the same chances of meeting an equally nice woman to marry. But considering things the way Olivier did produces a cancellation of the negative emotion of not ending up at his preferred destination, as he now sees the whole story. Narrating our life in a positive way triggers emotions based on the sum of several events, and not each of them individually. When emotions are all positive, then it is better to consider them separately. But when emotions are a mixture of good and bad news, then it is better to consider them jointly, so that the positive cancels the negative before loss aversion hits. The idea of mental accounting for the evaluation of good and bad news was introduced by Richard Thaler of the University of Chicago Booth School of Business.[15]

Religious people see their lives as a meaningful journey, where every action counts. We do not claim here that nonreligious people cannot have meaningful lives, but they need to find a way to see that what they do counts in one way or another.

It is believed that mathematicians tend to be interesting, and sometimes odd, characters. John von Neumann was one such character. Some say that he was the brightest mathematician of the twentieth century. As a child prodigy, he had a photographic memory so powerful that it seemed almost preternatural. Using his great intellect, he soon became famous for his pioneering ideas on electronic digital computers, as well as for his work on mathematical logic and on quantum mechanics.

His accomplishments got the attention of the U.S. government, and he ended up taking part in the Manhattan Project to develop the atomic bomb. One of his greatest interests, however, was in game theory, a fascination that began while he was running the drinking circles of Princeton University, when he realized he was not a very good poker player.

In his early fifties, the prime of his career as a researcher and consultant, he was diagnosed with prostate cancer, which had already metastasized and spread to his bones. He passed away a couple of years later. During that time, he could not accept the fact that this brilliant mind of his was deteriorating, and he was known to scream uncontrollably in terror during the night. Even though von Neumann had an unquestionable intelligence, it was not able to keep him from such suffering and, in fact, led him to take a very harsh perspective toward death.

Far away from von Neumann's reality, in a very different part of the world and at another time, lived Bhagawhandi, a nineteen-year-old Indian girl, who suffered from a malignant brain tumor that was diagnosed when she was only seven. In his nonfiction book *The Man Who Mistook His Wife for a Hat,* Oliver Sacks shares the story of how the tumor went into remission while she was growing up, but when she was eighteen, it flared up again, moving to her temporal lobe. She had to be put on steroids. In spite of her deteriorating condition, she always had a faint glint in her eyes and a gentle smile on her face.

While in the deep, yet vivid, dream states that accompanied the growth of her tumor, the girl began to relive her childhood, remembering scenes from her village and its surroundings, with familiar landscapes and faces of people who were close to her. At a time when her life was ticking away, these memories offered her comfort instead of stress and sadness. All she had at that moment were her memories, and that is what made her happy, making her extremely peaceful when facing the end of her life.

"I am dying, I am going home. I am going back to where I came from—you might call it my return," she told Sacks just before passing away.

The contrast between the two stories demonstrates how a happy state of mind is possible even in the most difficult of circumstances. Indeed, happiness resides in the mind. But the story also shows how elusive and difficult it can be to control happiness. It takes Buddhist monks and other religious devotees years of training to create a happy refuge in the mind. Nonetheless, the rest of us seem convinced that changing external circumstances—making money, buying stuff, and showing off—is what will make us happier.

Happiness is the state of mind that comes from feeling that you are no longer yearning for some unmet need. Nevertheless, we have a proclivity for manufacturing needs regardless of how much we have. For happiness to bloom, we need to see the sky as partly sunny, the glass as half full, and our lives as largely prosperous.

HAPPINESS IN ACTION

Every day, reframe at least one experience from negative to positive. For example, if a package you've been waiting for hasn't arrived yet, rather than getting upset, focus on how amazing it is that this package can travel across the country or around the world so (relatively) quickly.

CHAPTER 12

Living within the Laws of Happiness

The Constitution only gives people the right to pursue happiness. You have to catch it yourself.
　—Benjamin Franklin

Think of the myriad of activities one could engage in, or the thousands of products one could buy. How do these possibilities translate into emotions, feelings, and ultimately happiness?

We postulate that happiness is the sum total of positive and negative moment-happiness. A pleasant emotion leads to positive moment-happiness (a flirting glance from an attractive man or woman, or eating ice cream on a hot day), while a negative emotion (getting reprimanded by the boss) leads to a negative moment-happiness. We have proposed a set of general laws that govern most emotions. Based on these laws, we have constructed our fundamental equation of happiness:

HAPPINESS *is an S-curve of*
REALITY *minus* SHIFTING EXPECTATIONS

The equation says that happiness depends on what you get (reality) relative to what you want (expectations). The happiness S-curve accounts for loss aversion, diminishing sensitivity, and satiation. We have presented three ways in which expectations change: social comparison, adaptation, and reframing.

EXPECTATIONS SHIFT *depending on*
WHAT OTHERS GET,
WHAT I GOT IN THE PAST, *and*
WHAT I CHOOSE TO COMPARE.

The fundamental equation of happiness is the same, but there are different ways to operate the equation. We have identified five types of goods; for each good the fundamental equation of happiness operates in somewhat different way. Here is the list of the five types of goods, sorted in terms of reliability to produce happiness (from most reliable to least).

1. *Basic:* Basic goods and activities are those that satisfy the needs of the body, the heart, and the mind and for which expectations do not shift. When consumed at a constant rate, both reality and expectations are flat lines, leaving a gap of happiness (or unhappiness) between the two. Rest, food, shelter, health, sex, companionship, and safety are examples of basic goods. These deliver assured happiness. If resources are very limited, then these needs should be attended to first.

   The elimination of poverty, creation of a world where all people have their basic needs met to a minimum, is to us a solid and worthwhile goal that transcends ideologies and religions.

   In modern societies a good fraction of the population has their basic needs satisfied to a minimum. Once one reaches this point, then pouring additional resources into basic goods becomes inefficient, as the returns per dollar or hour invested decrease due to satiation effects. Diverting resources across other types of goods can then increase happiness.

2. *Reframing:* Reframing activities are those that seek to modify the way we perceive reality and to moderate expectations. Reality can be seen in multiple ways. Reframing will allow you

to see the same reality in a new light, make broader comparisons, or stay detached from what you own, thus mitigating adaptation and the fear of loss. The happiness return of reframed activities is assured. Hence, they are as solid as basic goods. Reframing, however, requires time and effort. But as with basic goods, there are diminishing returns, and it is optimal to pursue reframing only up to a point.

3. *Cumulative:* Cumulative goods and activities are those for which reality is perceived to be stored in a bucket. When consumed at a constant rate, reality and expectations become two lines that increase in parallel, leaving a space of happiness between the two. Progressing toward goals, helping with causes that transcend us, learning some skill, or developing relationships are all ways to be happy by gradually filling buckets.

As discovered by Csíkszentmihályi, in a world where basic needs are satisfied, engagement in activities to achieve goals is the way to jailbreak the happiness equation.

Cumulative goods act as basic goods if the bucket does not break. But very few things are safe. Long-term relationships break down, loved ones fall sick or die, large companies go bankrupt, and belief in causes can be lost. The bucket that has provided happiness while being filled can go empty. This is the nature of life.

Hence, although a lot of happiness can be obtained from cumulative goods, a lot of unhappiness may come due to their loss.

4. *Adaptive:* Most goods and activities are adaptive, meaning that expectations shift toward reality and we begin to take them for granted. When adaptive goods are consumed at a constant rate, then happiness increases for a while, but soon it goes to zero. Hence, the fundamental equation of happiness tells us that happiness is an elusive goal. Most of the material goods, comforts, and technological advantages brought by our consumer

society are adaptive. An increase in reality delivers an immediate increase in happiness, until references catch up and happiness declines. Hence, we propose the "less-to-more" recipe to manage expectations wisely and avoid their uncontrolled escalation. Consuming adaptive goods in a less-to-more fashion produces a constant stream of happiness, similar to that associated with basic and cumulative goods.

Adaptive goods are risky if one cannot keep up with expenses. Because they must be managed very wisely, adaptive goods are less reliable in producing happiness than basic and cumulative goods and reframing.

5. ***Social Comparison:*** Social comparison goods are those that we buy to imitate others or to look good in front of others. We cannot escape from comparing ourselves to others, as others are an important source of reference. Positive social comparison does yield happiness, in the same way that negative social comparison yields unhappiness. But we do not have full control of the base of comparison, as others' lifestyle is a moving target. Hence, as a source of happiness, it is not fully under our control. To maximize your own happiness, you should choose social groups that are a good fit, cultivate an attitude of admiration, and avoid ostentation.

Our five-fold classification of goods and activities is rooted in the basic psychology of emotions. This classification can be made operational mathematically. It tells us the return in happiness we are supposed to expect from pouring resources into each type of good, as dictated by the six laws of happiness.

A complex experience such as a vacation may include all five types of components. A vacation will have basic components that contribute to happiness: rest, good food, and peace of mind. However, a vacation also has adaptive components: the comforts of the hotel, the gadgets of the car we rent, and other luxuries. These components will increase happiness only if they are better than our expectations.

A vacation also involves social comparison, which can affect happiness. How will this vacation look to others? How will they react when I tell them? Here, recall that others really don't care much where you go on vacation, but you will surely feel happier if you have a feeling of comparing favorably.

A vacation can have cumulative components as well. It will definitely help improve relationships with others, and that will increase the stock of love or friendship. Moreover, if the vacation is part of a plan or a collection, such as visiting sites from the Unesco World Heritage List, then it will contribute to fill up the bucket of "places to visit."

Finally, some types of vacation may help us reframe our lives as we compare our privileged position to those who lack necessities that we take for granted.

Each of the five types of goods needs to be operated in a particular way in order to maximize happiness. In our consumer society, a rational person can find happiness by trying to choose a high and constant level of basic goods and activities (social relationships, food, and rest), and being very selective in which habits to initiate, and when to initiate them. For example, make sure you get into the habit of going to expensive restaurants when you have the time and the money to afford the extra expense. Of the habits that one chooses to initiate, make sure you treat the habits well, and plan always to go from less to more.

On top of that, why not choose the right pond of social comparison? When it comes to comparison, try to focus on those dimensions where you would have an advantage? Next, make sure the activities you engage in are stored in the form of stable relationships, long-term goals, learning experiences, and collectibles. Seek challenges and set goals in your life and work to foster a sense of personal growth. Or store your actions by, for example, contributing to projects and missions that are enduring.

Finally, spend some fixed time on reframing activities. As explained by the Buddhist monk Matthieu Ricard, "We are willing to spend many years acquiring education. We love to do jogging, fitness, and all kinds of things to remain beautiful. Yet, we spend surprising little time taking care of what matters the most: the way our minds function, which is the ultimate thing that determines the quality of our experience."[1]

When we optimize our fundamental equation, we find that the more adaptive the good, the higher the speed of adaptation, the longer we should delay the initiation of consumption. If the speed of adaptation is too fast, then we may want to skip indulging altogether. On the opposite end, as we lower the speed of adaptation, making it close to zero, we find the basic goods. The less adaptive the good, the less the optimal consumption rate rises over time. When the speed of adaptation is zero, then the optimal consumption rate is constant over time. Easy enough! Cumulative goods and time spent in reframing behave much the same way as basic goods: the optimal consumption rate is approximately constant over time.

Finally, conspicuous goods are like basic goods, except that other people determine the basis of comparison. In this case, the optimal consumption rate for conspicuous goods is to maintain a *constant gap* between our consumption and that of the neighbors. This is obviously problematic if your neighbors have much more money than you have.

> *The optimal consumption rate of adaptive goods is increasing; the optimal consumption rate of basic goods, cumulative goods, and reframing activities is fairly constant over time; and the optimal consumption rate of conspicuous goods it to keep a constant distance with respect to the neighbors.*

Therefore, you must choose very carefully which kinds of goods will be more prevalent in your life. Since different kinds of goods have different speeds of adaptation, they can vary greatly in how much happiness they allow one to obtain. You can clearly maximize happiness by allocating more time and resources to those goods and experiences for which hedonic adaptation and social comparison are less important.[2]

And last but not least: Lots of happiness from anticipation and recall can be obtained by looking forward to the vacation, doing a few extraordinary things that create recall, and making sure that the spacing between one vacation and the next is sufficiently long to enhance enjoyment.

We can also add a bit of spice to life by seeking novelty and variety. Taking some time between consumption helps us fight the sensory numbness produced by satiation. Spacing out the important events in your life can improve your happiness, as you may fully savor the anticipation and recall of each event, and avoid satiation.

EMOTIONAL DIVERSIFICATION

Buddhist monks, as we know, are known for controlling their emotions through meditation and spiritual practices; and, indeed, they are happy. In Buddhist practice, desire is seen as a source of suffering, and therefore should be controlled. Are we then supposed to become monks, devoting 100 percent of our time to reframing? We do not propose such a radical view. Rather, if we think that certain practices can lower our expectations and allow us to gain a better perspective in life, then it might be optimal to devote *some time* to such practices.

Spiritual practices often require discipline and time. In our mathematical model, we add the possibility that through time devoted to such activities, one effectively controls the rise of expectations. The result is that there is an optimal amount of time to be devoted to personal improvement and spiritual practices. However, if we behave like monks, and spend too much time introspecting, we may begin to ignore work, family, or social life. Some people choose to concentrate this optimal time for spiritual practices into one annual retreat, which may last for several days.

All the five types of goods are valid ways to reach happiness. But each good and activity we initiate suffers from diminishing returns. Hence, it is optimal to diversify and collect happiness from multiple goods and activities.

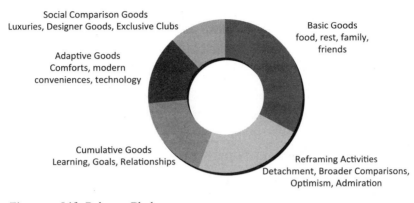

Social Comparison Goods
Luxuries, Designer Goods, Exclusive Clubs

Basic Goods
food, rest, family,
friends

Adaptive Goods
Comforts, modern
conveniences, technology

Cumulative Goods
Learning, Goals, Relationships

Reframing Activities
Detachment, Broader Comparisons,
Optimism, Admiration

Figure 6. Life Balance Chakra

With limited budget of money and time, the smart thing to do is to carefully select the goods and activities we engage in. The five different types of goods are all valid in principle, as long as we understand how they function and their advantages, disadvantages, and dangers. In fact, due to the principle of diminishing returns, the five types of goods can be sought simultaneously.

In financial investments, the advantages of diversification are well known. Emotional investment is no different: we need to strike a proper life balance to achieve maximum total happiness. For example, we should not put all our resources (time, focus, and money) into the single goal of our professional life and ignore our personal life. Nothing is certain, and all the efforts poured into the professional life can be lost if that promotion does not arrive, or the company we have strived to build goes bankrupt.

The life balance chakra (figure 6) shows the balancing of the five categories of goods and activities to achieve harmony and happiness. The size of the pie is 100 percent, which represents our total resources of time. The pie is divided into five slices, corresponding to the time spent in basic, reframing, cumulative, adaptive, and social comparison goods and activities, respectively. A similar pie could be built for money, with each slice representing the percentage of budget allocated to these five types of goods.

Two things are important to notice in the chakra. First, if you increase one segment, for example, time devoted to your work, then it comes at the expense of some other segment (time left for family and friends, rest, or reframing activities). Second, the relative allocation of resources (time, money, and focus) to different segments in the chakra is continuously changing with our circumstances. Consider parenting as an example. A newborn baby requires a great deal of time and attention from the parents. As the baby grows, the priorities change but you still need to make time for helping with homework and sports. Once you become an empty nester, you may take up a new hobby such as painting or even accept a more demanding job that you have been postponing.

In our survey, we asked our subjects to estimate how much time they spent on various activities, not including work. It might be helpful to know the average time people spend on different activities. The subjects spend 33 percent of their available time on family, 20 percent on leisure, 15 percent on friends, another 15 percent on attaining goals, 10 percent on personal improvement, and the rest, 7 percent, on helping other people.

LIFE CHAKRA UNDER PRESENTISM

Lottery winners may not be happier, as researchers have found, but most of us continue to believe that winning the lottery will make us happy forever. A direct consequence of the Law of Presentism is that we do not correctly predict that as our wealth grows, our expectation levels will also shift upward. Expectations rise for two reasons. First, we become accustomed to a higher standard of living—a bigger house, a fancier car, or nicer hotels. Second, our social comparison level may go up. If we foresee all this, then we will use our increased wealth in a prudent way and fully account for rising expectation levels. Because of presentism, we fail to foresee the increases in expectation levels. Instead, we think that spending as much as possible as quickly as possible will maximize happiness (when it does not).

We will now illustrate, using a hypothetical example, how the Law of Presentism explains a big puzzle: Why do we believe that more money will buy us a lot more happiness than it actually does?

For most people, money is obtained by spending time at work, at some hourly salary rate. Thus, time buys money. However, time can buy happiness directly, by engaging in activities such as spending time with family and friends, resting, pursuing goals, personal improvement, and helping other people.

Suppose Adam can choose white chips and yellow chips each year, but the total number of white plus yellow chips must be 100. The budget of 100 represents Adam's total time. The time available can be divided between work, white chips, and personal life, yellow chips. For example, if he chooses 30 white chips and 70 yellow chips, then Adam must work 30 percent of the time and he has the remaining 70 percent of time left for his personal life. With each white chip Adam can buy worldly goods and services. Let us say that the conversion rate for each white chip is $1,000. Adam derives happiness from purchasing goods (white chips), as well as from spending time on fun activities (yellow chips).

Adam knows that many things that matter a lot for happiness are essentially purchased with time. Indeed, scholars at the Royal College of Surgeons in Ireland examined the reflections of terminally ill patients. They observed that most people, when looking back on their lives, regret not the things they did, but rather the things that they did not have the time or find the time to do.

In the beginning, Adam chooses 30 white chips, so he works 30 percent of the time and has an expendable income of $30,000. He buys a scooter, pays rent, buys food, and uses the money earned for vacation and other recreational activities. Adam is happy.[3] The next year, Adam again has a choice of the number of white chips and yellow chips. Adam now wants a motorcycle, a better computer, and a more powerful speaker system. He needs more white chips. So he opts for 35 white chips and 65 yellow chips. He is now working a bit harder (35 percent of the time) and has a bit less time for his personal life. But Adam is happy, as he can now enjoy the toys he has purchased. As each year goes by, Adam's expectations creep upward. He wants a more powerful and trendy motorcycle and wants to live in an upscale neighborhood. Adam then chooses 50 white chips and 50 yellow chips. He is thus working 50 percent of the time and has less time left for his personal life. Adam is still happy, but does feel a bit pressed for time for leisure and rest. Eventually, Adam finds himself choosing 60 white chips and 40 yellow chips.

Adam is now quite short of time for his personal life, and his professional life occupies a greater share of his time. He now feels that his life is out of balance, but he is unable to change his lifestyle, as he needs to support his higher standard of living, which now includes a membership in a country club and the ownership of a beach house.

Adam has found himself in a bind because he uses the rule:

PREDICTED HAPPINESS *equals*
FUTURE REALITY *minus* CURRENT EXPECTATIONS

Adam thought that every new purchase would bring him happiness. As we know, his expectations marched upward as well. The actual result was that the increase in happiness with each new purchase was short-lived.

So why doesn't Adam learn? It is possible that Adam may mistakenly believe that each new luxury will be a source of continuous and durable joy. He just does not get that he will become adapted to his new trendy motorcycle faster than he thinks. Suppose we put Adam's preferences through a computer, but now using the rule:

ACTUAL HAPPINESS *equals*
FUTURE REALITY *minus* FUTURE EXPECTATIONS

With the computer and the correct rule in hand, Adam will still choose more and more white chips as time passes, but the increase will be slow. In the optimal allocation, Adam will not be caught unaware in a predicament in which his actual happiness has dwindled. In fact, his realized total happiness in each period will gradually *increase* over time.

The dilemma we just presented shows that presentism makes us buy more adaptive goods than are optimal, at the expense of basic goods. A more general question is: what is the effect of presentism on our life balance chakra? Let's look at the five types of goods and activities, one by one.

1. *Basic:* Happiness from basic goods will be correctly predicted, as the belief that expectations do not change happens to be correct in this case. For example, if you expect that a warm shower after a long hike will be just as satisfying in the future as it is now, you're right.

2. *Reframing:* If we believe that expectations will not move, then why spend time trying to moderate these expectations? If we cannot imagine that other perspectives in life are possible, why spend time acquiring new viewpoints? Presentism will make us underpredict happiness from spending time nurturing the inner self, as we will not easily see the returns to these efforts.

3. *Cumulative:* Strangely enough, presentism will make us overpredict the happiness from cumulative activities and cause us to overindulge in them. If we think that expectations do not change, then accumulating reality is bound to give us plenty of happiness! It will, but expectations will also shift and we will obtain a bit less happiness than predicted. Although cumulative activities are a reliable source of happiness, we may in fact spend too much time on pursuing projects, goals, and learning skills, as opposed to enjoying life!

4. *Adaptive:* Here is where presentism takes the highest toll. Presentism makes us underestimate adaptation and perceive adaptive goods as basic. For example, you cannot wait until the new iPhone comes out, but after you have it for a few months you will feel about it the same way you do about your current

phone. We always overpredict the happiness we will derive from adaptive goods.

5. **Social Comparison:** Presentism makes us believe that fame, prestige, and power will provide a lasting boost to our happiness seismogram, and that the lack of these will provide lasting unhappiness. In reality, the social environment is likely to change more than anticipated: family and friends can succeed or fail in their business, fame comes and goes, and circumstances change. Presentism makes us think that happiness or unhappiness from social comparison is more stable than it turns out to be. Because of presentism, we fail to anticipate the rat race; if we strive to become better than others, then others also will try hard to outshine us. In a talk one of us gave on happiness, a wealthy member of the audience recounted: "What you said about social comparison is so true. A friend of mine brought a Ferrari. The next thing I did was to buy an Aston Martin." Therefore, presentism also makes us overpredict the happiness from our social comparison goods.

In the life balance chakra, the segments of the goods categories for which happiness is overpredicted (cumulative, adaptive, and social comparison goods) will be larger than before. The segment of reframing activities, where happiness is underpredicted, is greatly reduced. Finally, the segment of basic goods, where we correctly predict happiness, is also reduced. This is because the limited resources of time and money are redirected from basic goods and reframing to adaptive and conspicuous goods.

We should have courage to create a new reality that reflects a harmonious balance between personal and professional life. The choice of lifestyle should be made deliberately. Because of presentism, there will be a tendency to overwork and gravitate toward higher-paying, more demanding, and stressful jobs. Even Warren Buffett had to pause and rebalance his lifestyle to include twelve hours of bridge per week in his routine. With the choice of new reality, you will be able to do previously unthinkable things, like take a weekly bike ride with your daughter.

In a survey we asked people to indicate which factors they think would increase their happiness level. The factor that was cited the most was money, followed by improvements in relationships, job, health, and others.

Researchers have found that money indeed boosts happiness in the short term, but only 20 percent of this increase remains in the long run. Because of presentism, the impact of money looms larger and could lead to an imbalanced life chakra.

HAPPINESS IN ACTION

Use your electronic calendar or a diary to record how you spend your time for different activities during one week. Classify the activities in relevant categories, such as work, family, friends, rest and leisure, personal improvement, and helping other people. Once this is done, ask yourself on which of these activities you could spend *more* time to improve your happiness.

CHAPTER 13

Building a Happier Life

Habits form a second nature. —Jean-Baptiste Lamarck

Benjamin Franklin decided at a young age that he must cultivate virtue. He proceeded to design a plan in which he would practice each virtue (for example, temperance) every day for one week. He would make a note when he fell short and, he hoped, with practice, over time the incidences of infractions would diminish.

We use an analogous approach but with a focus on improving happiness. You must first realize that a happier life is a *choice*, something in your hands. Carefully examine your life and determine which factors are important to you. Most people want a job they enjoy, financial security, good health, and fulfilling relationships. But you must be proactive in moving toward the goals that are important to you. Eating right and exercising is not just a slogan if you want good health in the long run. You must come up with a plan for a healthier lifestyle, make choices consistent with your plan, and monitor your progress. With effort and determination, eating right and exercise will become a habit and you will be on the road to a healthier life. A similar game plan can be devised to achieve the ultimate objective: happiness.

With our laws of happiness in mind, we will adapt Benjamin Franklin's system. We have identified thirteen pillars of happiness that, with practice, will help you build a happier life. These thirteen pillars are:

TABLE 2

Keeping Track of the Happiness Pillars

Happiness Pillars		Mon	Tue	Wed	Thu	Fri	Sat	Sun
1	Meals							
2	Sleep							
3	Work							
4	Relationships							
5	Recreation							
6	Crescendo							
7	Social Comparison							
8	Glass Half Full							
9	Small Sips							
10	Cumulation							
11	Forgiveness							
12	Life Balance							
13	Learning to Love							

meals, sleep, work, relationships, recreation, crescendo, social comparison, glass half full, small sips, cumulation, forgiveness, life balance, and learning to love.

It is useful to have a table with a row for each of these thirteen pillars along with seven columns, one for each day of the week (see table 2). The system is to focus on one particular pillar for an entire week. The idea is to break the habits that produce negative emotions or unhappiness and acquire habits that produce positive emotions or happiness. By focusing on one pillar at a time you can devote more attention and effort to that pillar.

Brain researchers have discovered that when we develop new habits, new neural pathways are created. As we repeat the habit, the pathways become stronger and it becomes easier to maintain the habit. So we must stick to a new habit and repeat it on a regular basis till it becomes a part of our life. Old habits are worn into the hippocampus, which is probably why we have the proverb "old habits die hard."

After a week of practice, you move to another pillar and focus your attention on making improvements on this new pillar. You should keep an eye on the other pillars that you have practiced in previous weeks, but your concentration should be fixed on improving one pillar at a time.

When all pillars have been visited and practiced over a thirteen-week period, contemplate your progress and your resolution for improvement over the next cycle of thirteen weeks. Thus, over a year, you will have four cycles of practicing each of the thirteen pillars, and your happiness level will have improved.

Here is an itemized list of the thirteen pillars, with some descriptive items listed for each of them.

1. MEALS: be peaceful, show gratitude, avoid overeating and overdrinking, eat with friends

2. SLEEP: sleep in a comfortable bed, let in fresh air, cultivate a quiet mind, recover from sleep deprivation

3. WORK: make your commute more pleasant, improve your relationships with coworkers, become more engaged with your work

4. RELATIONSHIPS: nurture your relationships with your family and friends, avoid toxic interactions

5. RECREATION: engage in regular exercise, learn some fun skills such as music or painting

6. CRESCENDO: be frugal, postpone expenses, save the best for last

7. SOCIAL COMPARISON: avoid envy, be modest, celebrate others' successes, praise and give credit

8. GLASS HALF FULL: reframe, accept imperfections, emphasize positives

9. SMALL SIPS: space out your consumption, build craving, cultivate varied interests

10. CUMULATION: create meaning, set goals, fill the bucket

11. FORGIVENESS: avoid resentment, conciliate, seek pardon

12. BALANCE: find balance in your life among career, family, hobbies, and self-improvement

13. LEARNING TO LOVE: practice compassion, cultivate spirituality, help others

ENJOY YOUR MEALS

Let's begin with the first pillar: enjoying your meals. It may come as a surprise that we focus on meals as a means to build a happier life. In our theory, happiness is a sum total of positive and negative emotions. To cultivate positive emotions, we must first practice on some activity we do every day and possibly several times during the day. Eating is one such activity. Too many people eat hurried meals and do not create a peaceful environment or have the proper mental attitude to enjoy their meals. "Eat not to dullness; drink not to elevation" is good advice from Benjamin Franklin. But there is more to cultivating a positive mental attitude toward your food than simply its quantity. Learn to appreciate the color, smell, and taste of your food and engage in pleasant conversation with friends and family during the meal whenever possible. There will of course be days when there is a plane to catch or a meeting to attend when a hurried meal is the only possibility. Even in these instances, the experience of eating need not be mirthless.

Suppose you have three meals a day. Each day for the next week, allow yourself a star for each meal during which you had positive emotions and enjoyed the experience. On a perfect day, you would receive three stars. In the first days, you may not be able to record any stars at all. But as you improve your mental attitude and your gratitude for the food you have, it is quite possible that by the end of the week you will

TABLE 3

Keeping Track of the Meals Pillar

Happiness Pillars		Mon	Tue	Wed	Thu	Fri	Sat	Sun
MEALS: be peaceful, show gratitude, avoid overeating or overdrinking, eat with friends								
1	Meals		*		**	*	***	**
2	Sleep							
3	Work							
4	Relationships							
5	Recreation							
6	Crescendo							
7	Social Comparison							
8	Glass Half Full							
9	Small Sips							
10	Cumulation							
11	Forgiveness							
12	Life Balance							
13	Learning to Love							

be filling in three stars. (See the example in table 3.) Habit formation is not easy and you will indeed slip occasionally. But that is fine as long as you are making progress.

PLEASANT SLEEP

Most of us sleep an average of six to eight hours per night. A good night's sleep is essential to health and happiness. Make sure that your bedroom is conducive to restful sleep: comfortable bed and pillow, fresh air, and clean linens. With modern-day pressures, there will most likely be times when you do not get adequate sleep. On such occasions, have a plan to make up the sleep deficit on weekends or whenever the opportunity arises. There is a tendency, especially among young people, to squander this opportunity by partying all night long.

Besides the quantity of sleep, exercise and temperance when eating food (especially for supper) improve the quality of sleep. Just before bedtime, unclutter your mind or read a calming book. This practice will improve the quality of your sleep and possibly bring on pleasant dreams. Again, rate yourself from no star to three stars on the restfulness of the sleep you experience each day. In our definition, the pleasure of sleep adds to happiness. Similarly, a restless night or unpleasant dreams subtracts from happiness.

WORK

The single activity on which we spend perhaps the greatest amount of time is work. The first step to deriving happiness from work is to improve the quality of your commute. Walking to work, reading on a bus, or listening to music all help in creating a positive mood when you reach your workplace. If the commute is long, then you may want to listen to audio books, which will keep your attention away from the annoying traffic and noise. If you are careful in the selection of audio books, the commute will feel less onerous and even enjoyable.

You may consciously make an effort to improve your relationships with coworkers. Congenial relationships at work are not just good office politics: they boost positive emotions. Smile often, avoid trifling conversations, and be helpful to your coworkers, and they will reciprocate with a gentler attitude toward you.

Become more engaged with your work. No task is too small and all work performed earnestly gives a gift of joy. Find something challenging in what you do, neither too easy nor too difficult, so that your skills are exercised and your mind stays busy. Idleness and boredom are injurious to mental health.

RELATIONSHIPS

Family and friends can be a reliable source of happiness provided you have good relationships with them. Whatever the condition of your relationship with your family and friends is, you can always improve it. Eating a meal together, engaging in pleasant conversations, playing cards, or going on an outing are some ways to find joy in spending time with your family and friends.

Each of us probably has strong feelings about certain issues or topics. Discussing these topics can spice up conversations but often leads to unnecessary confrontations and hurt feelings. If the conversation cannot be kept upbeat, it is often better to avoid igniting a fire.

A Gallup poll revealed that Americans are happiest when they spend six to seven hours a day socializing. Not everyone has that much time to socialize. The good news is that even a modest amount of socialization increases happiness and decreases stress, worry, and unhappiness.

Visit your family, make new friends, join a book club, engage in pleasant conversations at your church or bridge club, and you will see a boost in your happiness.

Maintaining old relationships and making new friends requires active planning, such as making arrangements for lunch or dinner or planning weekend outings. The time spent actively planning will provide assured happiness and will probably be worth more than spending this time watching TV or idling.

RECREATION

Make time for regular exercise, learn some fun skills (sports, dance, painting, cooking), play music, or relax and read. You will see that stress and negative emotions give way to engagement, happiness, and positive emotions.

People enjoy recreation and intend to pursue it, but sometimes life gets in the way. Join a yoga class or a reading club to enforce the discipline. It will be easier to pursue the activity voluntarily once a habit is acquired and becomes a part of your daily routine.

CRESCENDO

A clear implication of our laws of happiness is that a rational person should not be extravagant when young and should control expectation levels by acquiring adaptive goods hesitantly. Too much conspicuous consumption (fancy cars, designer clothes, expensive vacations) early on leads to a rapid increase in expectations and it becomes difficult to maintain happiness in the future. You should plan consumption from less to more over time.

In daily life, practicing frugality, especially regarding the latest toy, is the way to tame expectations. One way to practice frugality is to avoid impulse buying. Postpone buying a new TV if your old TV is working fine. Why begin the habit of going out for expensive coffee every day? Look around and see if you can avoid waste or control expenses for meals and entertainment.

There is another way to take advantage of crescendo to boost happiness. Save the best for last, whether you are on vacation or on a simple outing with friends. For example, it is better to stay in more luxurious accommodations toward the end of a trip.

SOCIAL COMPARISON

Have you noticed that some people are happier than others? One secret of happy people is that they are content with what they have and do not envy others' fortune or fame. So next time you see a fancy convertible stopped next to your car, do not let your mind wander off on how wonderful life would be if you had that car. Actually, the person driving the convertible may not be as happy as you think. Unnecessary social comparisons are toxic to your mental health—avoid them.

Acquire the habit of not boasting and avoid showing off your fame and riches. When we make displays of property or skill, people feel jealousy and resentment. Others will admire you most if they see your modesty.

One good way to reduce envy is to practice praising others for their good deeds and accomplishments. You may start out by simply being kind and helpful to others. At work give credit to your coworkers, and in your personal life celebrate when good things happen to your friends. Over time, you will turn the envy upside down and your life will be filled with positive emotions.

GLASS HALF FULL

Bad things sometimes happen. Your car may break down or your child may fall sick. It is normal to be concerned in these situations. Remember, however, that Victor Frankl managed to endure the horror of a concentration camp with a positive attitude. Even though that is an extreme, you should develop the habit of looking for positive aspects and reframing situations to reduce the negative thoughts.

Recall the times when you were furious because your daughter spilled the orange juice, the plumbing in your house clogged, the bagel was burned, the car was not finished being repaired when promised, or you got a parking ticket. Do not let these small mishaps depress your happiness seismogram for long. Rage, worry, irritation, frustration, despair, and vengeance are negative emotions that wreak havoc on your mental health.

How can you ignore the negatives and focus on the positives in life? Every day, at the end of the day, think of a positive and rewarding experience that you had during the day. An appreciation of positive moments in life is a start toward cultivating positive emotions and diverting attention from negative emotions.

SMALL SIPS

Too much of even good things dulls our senses and reduces enjoyment. Just think about the savory turkey dinner at your mom's house that you look forward to every year. After the big meal, you do not even want to entertain the idea of another turkey meal a week later. Some time must elapse before you can enjoy another turkey meal.

Variety adds zest to life. The same experience repeated again and again in a short time interval, even if it is skydiving, becomes tedious. A simple way to conquer satiation is to let some time elapse so you enjoy the repetition of the activity. If you cultivate a wide range of interests, then you can rotate among activities and will not fall prey to the boredom that excessive repetition breeds.

CUMULATION

There must be pleasures past the Reach of Sense,
Some nobler Source must Happiness dispense
—Anonymous, "An Essay on Happiness," 1737

A meaningful life is indicative of a good life. To see meaning and purpose in our lives, we should make sure that our actions and activities get stored in a metaphorical bucket. We should set goals and make progress toward those goals. A goal can be anything from planting a rose bush to losing ten pounds of weight, writing a poem, preparing for a marathon, or donating money to a charity. The key is to recognize that each day you are making progress toward a goal, like filling a bucket with water.

At work do not fret over a deadline or rush to get a memo out. Instead, think of work as progress toward a goal. In any project, whether it is designing a Web site or organizing a conference, the initial state of affairs may be disorderly. With steady progress and a cumulative view, there will be satisfaction when the project is completed. Each day at work and at home, practice the habit of looking at your "bucket" and appreciating how far you have come, rather than just what you have accomplished that day.

FORGIVENESS

If you learn to forgive, you will be healthier and happier. Small disagreements, hurts, insults, and wrongs are "cumulative bads" that cause mental anguish and pain. Forgiveness puts an abrupt end to any resentment and restores mental peace.

You must actively choose to forgive the person who has wronged you, spoken harshly to you, or offended you. You will find peace and may even see a change in the future behavior of the person who caused you the suffering.

If you have wronged someone, even unintentionally, then seek forgiveness and express sincere sorrow and regret. There is no guarantee that others will forgive you, but asking for pardon will soften their negative feelings toward you.

Each day, practice forgiveness by focusing on a coworker, family member, neighbor, or friend. The resentment of your grudge may resurface, but keep working on controlling it until it vanishes altogether and you have reestablished the relationship that was damaged.

BALANCE

We should seek a harmonious balance between our personal and professional lives. Too many of us work too hard and compromise our family and social life.

So go ahead and make plans to see your friends for dinner or a movie, have an outing with your spouse, or go to the zoo with your children. These activities are joyful in themselves, and they also create emotional diversification. If, on occasion, things do not go well at work, then a happy personal life acts as a buffer to stress at work.

Develop hobbies and interests outside of work. Get to know and appreciate outdoor activities and nature. Get involved in a community, religious, or political organization. When you have a wide range of interests, then a loss of any one activity will not cause much harm, as you can fall back on the others.

LEARNING TO LOVE

Perhaps the single most important ingredient in cultivating positive emotions is love. Love for your children, spouse, family, and friends is a delight in itself. But if you learn to love, then it will be easy for you to develop compassion and kindness toward all human beings.

In daily practice, develop your deeply rooted instinct to love. It may be easier to focus on one person, activity, or cause. For a mother, it is natural to focus on her child, whom she is inclined to love anyway. For some people, it may be love of God achieved through religious practice, and for others it may be love for the environment and nature.

Domestic happiness is increased by love. Researchers have found that helping others improves your own well-being. But love is the seed of the desire to help. So if you have learned to love, then happiness will surely knock on your door.

CONCLUDING THOUGHTS

How do we mesmerize the butterfly of our mind to make it stay on the flowers of positive states of being? Is the secret of happiness rooted in control of our mind, emotions, and behaviors? Our goal throughout this book has been to show you how to step out and watch the butterfly from the outside. It is in these little moments of retreat and freedom that happiness has a chance to blossom. The control lever for attaining happiness is in your hands.

No one saves us but ourselves. No one can and no one may. We ourselves must walk the path. —Buddha

NOTES

INTRODUCTION

1. Witt, A. (2005, January 30). Rich man, poor man. *Washington Post,* p. W14.

2. Zoroya, G. (2004, February 12). One wild ride for jackpot winner. *USA Today.*

3. McMahon, D.M. (2006). *Happiness: A History.* New York: Grove Press, p. 64.

4. Bentham, J. (1789). *An Introduction to the Principles of Morals and Legislation* (1996 edition), ed. J.H. Burns and H.L.A. Hart. Oxford: Clarendon Press, chapter 1. Emphasis in the original.

5. Mill, J.S. (1861). *Utilitarianism* (1993 edition), ed. G. Williams. London: Everyman; Russell, B. (1930). *The Conquest of Happiness.* London: George Allen and Unwin.

6. James, W. (1884). What is an emotion? *Mind* 9: 188–205; Maslow, A. (1964). *Religions, Values, and Peak-Experiences.* Columbus: Ohio State University Press.

7. Easterlin, R. (2001). Income and happiness: Towards a unified theory. *Economic Journal* 111: 465–484. See also Easterlin, R. (1974). Does economic growth improve the human lot? In *Nations and Households in Economic Growth: Essays in Honor of Moses Abramovitz,* ed. P.A. David and M.W. Reder, pp. 89–125. New York: Academic Press.

8. Brickman, P., D. Coates, and R. Janoff-Bullman. (1978). Lottery winners and accident victims: Is happiness relative? *Journal of Personality and Social Psychology* 37: 917–927.

9. Lykken, D. (1999). *Happiness: What Studies on Twins Show Us about Nature, Nurture, and the Happiness Set Point.* New York: Golden Books.

10. Adapted from www.firstpeople.us. Native American Indian Legends—Two Wolves—Cherokee.

I. MEASURING HAPPINESS

1. Ed Diener is the Joseph R. Smiley Distinguished Professor of Psychology at the University of Illinois, Urbana-Champaign. He was the president of both the International Society of Quality of Life Studies and the Society of Personality and Social Psychology. He was the editor of the *Journal of Personality and Social Psychology* and of the *Journal of Happiness Studies.* He has more than 240 publications, including about 190 on the psychology of well-being. His research interests are the measurement of well-being; temperament and personality influences on well-being; theories of well-being; income and well-being; and cultural influences on well-being.

2. Diener, E., L. Seidlitz, and E. Sandvik. (2006). Subjective well-being: The convergence and stability of self-report and non-self-report measures. *Journal of Personality* 61(3): 317–342.

3. The World Database of Happiness, a project started in 1980, is a database covering some fifteen thousand scientific findings on happiness, of which about five thousand are distributional findings (on how happy people are) and another ten thousand correlational findings (on what goes with more and less happiness). It is based at the Department of Sociology at the University of Rotterdam. The World Values Survey, a nonprofit network of social scientists coordinated by a central body based in Stockholm, has surveyed the basic values and beliefs of more than eighty different societies all over the planet.

4. Biswas-Diener, R., J. Vitterso, and E. Diener. (2005). Most people are pretty happy, but there is cultural variation: The Inughuit, the Amish and the Maasai. *Journal of Happiness Studies* 6: 205–226. This article supports the claim that most people are happy.

5. Blanchflower, D. G., and A. J. Oswald. (2008). Is well-being U-shaped over the life cycle? *Social Science and Medicine* 66: 1733–1749.

6. Wolfers, J., and B. Stevenson. (2008). Happiness inequality in the United States. Institute for the Study of Labor (IZA), discussion paper 3624.

7. Oishi, S., E. Diener, and R. E. Lucas. (2007). The optimum level of well-being: Can people be too happy? *Perspectives on Psychological Science* 2(4): 346–360.

8. Inglehart, R., and H.-D. Klingemann. (2000). Genes, culture, democracy, and happiness. In *Culture and Subjective Well-Being*, ed. E. Diener and E. M. Suh, pp. 165–183. Cambridge, MA: MIT Press.

9. Bok, D. (2010). *The Politics of Happiness*. Princeton, NJ: Princeton University Press.

10. Keynote address at the first World Congress on Positive Psychology, Philadelphia, June 2009.

11. Speech available on YouTube. Search for "Robert F. Kennedy challenges Gross Domestic Product."

12. Gross National Happiness: The Centre for Bhutan Studies. See www.grossnationalhappiness.com.

13. A good starting point to learn about the literature on culture and happiness is the book *Culture and Subjective Well-Being*, edited by Ed Diener and Eunkook Suh.

14. Daniel Kahneman, the Eugene Higgins Professor of Psychology and Public Affairs at Princeton University, explored the field of behavioral finance and hedonic psychology and won the 2002 Nobel Prize in Economic Sciences. Kahneman is responsible for key contributions in the field of well-being measurements, as his work explores the day reconstruction method. The view we present here agrees with Kahneman, D. (2000). Experienced utility and objective happiness: A moment-based approach. In Choices, Values and Frames, ed. D. Kahneman and A. Tversky, pp. 673–692. New York: Cambridge University Press and the Russell Sage Foundation. See Kahneman's TED talk with the title "The Riddle of Experience vs. Memory."

15. Kahneman, D., A. B. Krueger, D. A. Schkade, N. Schwarz, and A. A. Stone. (2004). A survey method for characterizing daily life experience: The day reconstruction method. *Science* 306(5702): 1776–1780.

16. Mihály Csíkszentmihályi, a Hungarian, is the C. S. and D. J. Davidson Professor of Psychology and Management and the director of the Quality of Life Research Center at the Claremont Graduate University. He is one of the leading names in positive psychology. Among his interests are creativity and innovation, and exploring the concept of flow, a condition in which a human being is completely immersed in the activity he or she is performing and experiencing happiness. He introduced the concept in his book *Flow: The Concept of Optimal Experience* (New York: Harper & Row, 1990). In general terms, flow is the moment in which you lose track of time—for instance, when a musician is playing an instrument or when a ballerina is taken by the rhythms of the music.

17. Killingsworth, M. A., and D. T. Gilbert. (2010). A wandering mind is an unhappy mind. *Science* 339(12): 932.

18. Daly, M., and D. Wilson. (2006). Keeping up with the Joneses and staying ahead of the Smiths: Evidence from suicide data. Federal Reserve Bank of San Francisco, working paper series, 2006–12.

19. David Snowdon is an epidemiologist and a professor of neurology at the Sanders-Brown Center on Aging at the University of Kentucky. He directed the Nun Study in collaboration with the School Sisters of Notre Dame in the United States.

20. Paul Ekman is a professor of psychology in the Department of Psychiatry at the University of California, San Francisco. Ekman did pioneering research in the 1960s exploring happiness in human beings. He visited an isolated population in Papua New Guinea and found that our feelings and emotions, and the way we express them, are natural to the human being, not learned or acquired as once believed. See Ekman, P. (2003). *Emotions Revealed*. New York: Henry Holt.

21. The *Duchenne smile* is what scientists call the true smile, which engages the muscles around the eyes as well as those around the mouth. These muscles are believed to be involuntary, which means that they move only in the presence of real enjoyment. Facial expression, electroencephalography (EEG), and self-report of subjective emotional experience were recorded while subjects individually watched both pleasant and unpleasant films. The name is derived from the man who first studied the muscles of the face, the French neurologist Guillaume Benjamin Amand Duchenne.

22. Bartels, A., and S. Zeki. (2000). The neural basis of romantic love. *Neuroreport* 11(17): 3829–3834.

23. Richard Davidson is a professor of neuroscience at the University of Wisconsin, Madison, where he directs the Waisman Laboratory for Brain Imaging and Behavior. Among Davidson's research areas are emotion and cerebral asymmetry; functional brain imaging studies (positron emission tomography, or PET, and fMRI) of depression and anxiety disorders; and individual differences in functional activation of emotions.

24. In a study by Urry et al., eighty-four right-handed individuals (drawn from the Wisconsin Longitudinal Study) provided answers to questions on positive and negative affect, and measures of both hedonic well-being (using global life satisfaction scores) and eudaimonic well-being (measured by questions on autonomy, determination, interest and engagement, aspirations and motivation, and a sense of meaning, direction, or purpose in life). See Urry, H., J. Nitschke,

I. Dolski, D. Jackson, K. Dalton, C. Mueller, M. Rosenkranz, C. Ryff, B. Singer, and R. Davidson. (2004). Making a life worth living: Neural correlates of well-being. *Psychological Science* 15(6): 367–372.

2. DEFINING HAPPINESS

1. James Russell started by exploring the topic of how emotions are influenced by the environment, which then led him to study how emotions in general can be described and assessed. He also proposed a map of emotions in Russell, J. (1980). A circumplex model of affect. *Journal of Personality and Social Psychology* 39: 1161–1178.

2. Psychologists actually use three dimensions to describe emotions, namely, pleasure, arousal, and dominance (PAD). *Dominance* refers to the capacity to exert control. We chose the first two for ease of exposition. References are Russell (1980); Watson, D., and A. Tellegen. (1985). Toward a consensual structure of mood. *Psychological Bulletin* 98: 219–235; Larsen, R., and E. Diener. (1992). Promises and problems with the circumplex model of emotion. *Review of Personality and Social Psychology* 13: 25–59; and Bradley, M.M., and P.J. Lang. (1994). Measuring emotion: The self-assessment manikin and the semantic differential. *Journal of Behavioral Therapy and Experimental Psychiatry* 25(1): 49–59.

3. The map includes the fifteen basic emotions listed by Richard Lazarus in his classic work *Emotion and Adaptation.* See Lazarus, R. (1991). *Emotion and Adaptation.* New York: Oxford University Press. Richard Lazarus (1922–2002) was a professor emeritus of psychology at the University of California, Berkeley.

4. A seismogram is a graph output by a seismograph. It is a record of the ground motion at a measuring station.

5. The area rule is not the only possibility to define total happiness. Suppose that, given a large set of happiness recordings, each being a feasible way in which one's life could unfold, one were to have the time and patience to rank them from most preferred to least preferred. Such sorting could be based on total happiness experienced, as well as on the variety of emotions experienced and the timing of their arrival. Suppose one could sort the happiness seismograms from better to worse. Then we could attach a numerical score to each happiness recording: a higher score to the more preferred, and a lower score to the less preferred. Such a numerical score would be a quantitative definition of total happiness. The area under the seismogram is a particular example of such a score. The mathematical economist Gerard Debreu showed in the 1960s that it is possible to associate a quantitative score with a qualitative pairwise ranking

of objects, even if there are infinitely many such objects. Here, the objects are possible happiness seismograms.

6. A theoretical justification for using the area under the curve as a measure of total utility (happiness) is provided in Kahneman, D., P. Wakker, and R. Sarin. (1997). Back to Bentham? Explorations of experienced utility. *Quarterly Journal of Economics* 112(2): 375–405.

7. Passage from the "Appendix on Hedonimetry," pp. 98–102, in Edgeworth, F. Y. (1881). *Mathematical Psychics: An Essay on the Application of Mathematics to the Moral Sciences.* London: C. Kegan Paul & Co. *Mathematical Psychics* is one of the great books in the history of economics.

8. This is one of the chapters in Elster, J., and G. Loewenstein, eds. (1992). *Choice over Time.* New York: Russell Sage Foundation. A sequel to this landmark book is Loewenstein, G., D. Read, and R. F. Baumeister, eds. (2003). *Time and Decision: Economic and Psychological Perspectives on Intertemporal Choice.* New York: Russell Sage Foundation.

9. Loewenstein G. (1987). Anticipation and the valuation of delayed consumption. *Economic Journal* 97(387): 666–684. See also Loewenstein, G. (1988). Frames of mind in intertemporal choice. *Management Science* 34: 200–214.

10. Miller, G. (2008). Neuroscience: Hippocampal firing patterns linked to memory recall. *Science* 321: 1280b–1281b.

11. Fredrickson, B., and D. Kahneman. (1993). Duration neglect in retrospective evaluations of affective episodes. *Journal of Personality and Social Psychology* 65: 45–55.

3. THE FIRST LAW OF HAPPINESS

1. Isaac Newton (1643–1727), an English mathematician, physicist, astronomer, philosopher, alchemist, and theologian, is the author of *Philosophie Naturalis Principia Mathematica,* in which he described universal gravitation and the three laws of motion, which today are the basis of engineering.

2. Hemenway, D., and S. Solnick. (1998). Is more always better? A survey on positional concerns. *Journal of Economic Behavior and Organization* 37(3): 373–383.

3. McGuire, M., M. Raleigh, and G. Brammer. (1982). Sociopharmacology. *Annual Review of Pharmacological Toxicology* 22: 643–661.

4. Leon Festinger (1919–1989): the American psychologist who became famous for his 1957 book *Theory of Cognitive Dissonance,* in which the basic idea is that individuals need to have balance in their thoughts as well as in their actions to avoid uncomfortable psychological tension, resulting in their changing their

beliefs and behaviors. Though this was his greatest contribution to psychology, he also proposed the social comparison theory, in which people tend to compare themselves with others around them to evaluate their own opinions and desires.

5. Bertrand Russell (1872–1970): the British historian, mathematician, philosopher, logician, and pacifist, known for making philosophy accessible to the general public. In 1950 he was awarded the Nobel Prize in Literature for a variety of significant writings on humanitarian ideals and freedom of thought.

6. Medvec, V., S. Madey, and T. Gilovich. (1995). When less is more: Counterfactual thinking and satisfaction among Olympic medalists. *Journal of Personality and Social Psychology* 69(4): 603–610.

7. Baumann, D., R. Cialdini, and D. Kenrick. (1981). Altruism as hedonism: Helping and self gratification as equivalent responses. *Journal of Personality and Social Psychology* 40: 1039–1046.

4. THE SECOND LAW OF HAPPINESS

1. Daniel Kahneman used this cold-hot example during his Nobel Prize lecture, which you can watch at www.nobelprize.org.

2. Schultz, W. (2000). Multiple reward signals in the brain. *Nature Reviews Neuroscience* 1: 199–207.

3. Van Praag, B. M. S., and A. Ferrer-i-Carbonell. (2008). *Happiness Quantified: A Satisfaction Calculus Approach*. Revised edition. Oxford: Oxford University Press. Chapter 8 studies the influence of the reference group. Quotation is from page 162. The data supporting the 80 percent adaptation rule is given in Van Praag, B. M. S., and A. Ferrer-i-Carbonell. (2008). Do people adapt to changing circumstances? The discussion is not finished yet. Working paper, Erasmus University and the Institute for Economic Analysis (CSIC).

5. THE THIRD LAW OF HAPPINESS

1. Nico Frijda's work titled *The Emotions* (New York: Cambridge University Press, 1986) reviews the research on emotions. Frijda argues that emotions can be described in terms of a set of laws. See Frijda, N. (1988). The laws of emotions. *American Psychologist* 43(5): 349–358.

2. Chen, M. K., Lakshminarayanan, V., and Santos, L. R. (2006). How Basic Are Behavioral Biases? Evidence from Capuchin Monkey Trading Behavior. *Journal of Political Economy* 114(3): 517–537.

3. Visit www.stickk.com. See also Ayres, Ian (2010). *Carrots and Sticks: Unlock the Power of Incentives to Get Things Done*. New York: Bantam Books.

4. Thaler, R., and S. Benartzi. (2004). Save more tomorrow: Using behavioral economics to increase employee saving. *Journal of Political Economy* 112(1): S164–S187.

6. THE FOURTH LAW OF HAPPINESS

1. This function, known as the value function, was proposed by Kahneman and Tversky in the context of risky choice. It was later applied to riskless situations. See Tversky, A., and D. Kahneman. (1991). Loss aversion in riskless choice: A reference-dependent model. *Quarterly Journal of Economics* 106(4): 1039–1061.

2. This adaptation equation has been studied since 1970. Economists use it to find optimal investment and consumption strategies under habit formation. The implications for marketing and consumer behavior have been developed by business school professors such as Luc Wathieu and ourselves. Pollak, R. (1970). Habit Formation and Dynamic Demand Functions. *Journal of Political Economy* 78(4): 745–763. Sundaresan, S. (1989). Intertemporally Dependent Preferences and the Volatility of Consumption and Wealth. *Review of Financial Studies* 3(1): 73–89. Constantinides, G. M. (1990). Habit Formation: A Resolution of the Equity Premium Puzzle, *Journal of Political Economy* 98(3): 519–543. Wathieu, L. (1997). Habits and the anomalies in intertemporal choice. *Management Science* 43(11): 1552–1563; and Wathieu, L. (2004). Consumer Habituation. *Management Science* 50(5): 587–596. Rozen, K. (2010). Foundations of Intrinsic Habit Formation. *Econometrica* 78(4): 1341–1373.

3. Let $R(t)$ and $E(t)$ denote the level of reality and expectations at time t, respectively. Given the level of reality set by Jack, $R(t)$, $t = 1, 2, \ldots, 50$, and initial expectations $E(1) = 0$, expectations move according to the law:

$E(t+1) = E(t) + \text{Speed of Adaptation} \times (R(t) - E(t))$, $t = 1, \ldots, 50$.

Denoted by $H()$ is the happiness S-curve. The happiness seismogram takes the following values over time:

Happiness $(t) = H(R(t) - E(t))$,

The happiness S-curve, $H(R-E)$, that we have used, as typed in Excel, is:

$= 10 * \text{IF}(R-E<0, -\lambda, 1) * (1 - \text{EXP}(-(\text{ABS}(R-E)^{0.8})/2))$.

The value of 10 is a scaling factor for the units of happiness, the term $\text{IF}(R-E<0, -\lambda, 1)$ accounts for loss aversion, and we set $\lambda = 2$ (losses are twice as painful as gains), and the expo-power function 1-EXP(-(ABS(R-E)^0.8)/2) accounts for diminishing sensitivity. The coefficients 0.8 and 2 are the relative and absolute part or diminishing sensitivity. See Holt, C., and S. Laury. (2002). Risk aversion and incentive effects. *American Economic Review* 92(5): 1644–1655. The relative part of 0.8 is fixed and well established empirically. The absolute scaling of 2 needs to be adjusted to the units by which reality is measured.

4. The happiness S-curve is scaled so that it takes value six when reality minus expectations is two. Hence, if the speed of adaptation were zero, then spending two coins per month would produce six units of happiness per period, and a total happiness of three hundred. Because of adaptation, the attainable happiness is smaller.

5. In day 12, Jack realizes that his expectations are too high and he is running out of budget. The strategy that optimizes happiness from day 12 to day 50 consists of drastically reducing consumption first, thus lowering expectations, and then gradually increasing consumption. Specifically, the optimal plan consists of consuming 0 during the next 12 days, then 1 during 12 days, 2 during 6 days, 3 during 4 days, and 4 during 4 days.

6. Allen Parducci proposes a different mechanism, called the contextual theory. The claim is that the range of happiness one can experience depends on one's past experiences. A wider range of happiness and unhappiness experienced in the past will increase the range. See Parducci, A. (1995). *Happiness, Pleasure, and Judgment: The Contextual Theory and Its Applications.* Mahwah, NJ: Lawrence Erlbaum Associates.

7. Huxley, A. (1932). *Brave New World.* New York: Harper.

7. THE FIFTH LAW OF HAPPINESS

1. We take the basic formula *Happiness = H(Reality − Expectations)*, where *H()* is the usual S-curve of happiness. To account for satiation levels, we let S denote the satiation level, and propose that happiness is the increment in the S-curve from the satiation level on. In formula,

Happiness = H($\mathbf{R} - \mathbf{E} + \mathbf{S}$) − H($\mathbf{S}$),

Where *S*, the *Satiation Level,* is a sum of past consumption, weighted by its recency. A possible rule to determine the satiation level is the following:

New $\mathbf{S}$ = Speed of Satiation × ($\mathbf{R} - \mathbf{E} + \mathbf{S}$)

Here, the speed of satiation is a number between zero and one. If the speed is zero, then there is no buildup of satiation. If the speed of satiation is one, then the satiation level is the sum of consumption above expectations so far. When reality is equal to expectations, then the satiation level decays at the rate given by the speed of adaptation.

2. Smith, A. (1776). *The Wealth of Nations* Reprint. New York: Random House (p. 183).

3. Pohl, F. (April 1954). The Midas plague. *Galaxy Science Fiction.*

4. Baucells, M., and R. Sarin. (2007). Satiation in discounted utility. *Operations Research* 55(1): 170–181.

5. Brickman, P., D. Coates, and R. Janoff-Bullman. (1978). Lottery winners and accident victims: Is happiness relative? *Journal of Personality and Social Psychology* 37: 917–927.

6. Johnson, S. (1856). *Rasselas.* Philadelphia: Willis P. Hazard.

7. Baucells, M., and R. Sarin. (2010). Predicting utility under satiation and habit formation. *Management Science* 56(2): 286–301.

8. Rosaldo, R. I. (1989). *Culture and Truth: The Remaking of Social Analysis.* Boston: Beacon Press.

9. To help nonprofit group, woman eats on a dollar a day. *San Diego Union-Tribune,* May 12, 2008.

10. Flannery, B. A., J. R. Volpicelli, and H. M. Pettinati. (1999). Psychometric properties of the Penn Alcohol Craving Scale. *Alcoholism: Clinical and Experimental Research* 23: 1289–1295.

11. Anton, R. (1999). What is craving? Models and implications for treatment. *Alcohol Research and Health* 23(3): 165–173.

12. Rozin, P., E. Levine, and C. Stoess. (1991). Chocolate craving and liking. *Appetite* 3(17): 199–212. See also Yanovski, S. (2003). Sugar and fat: Cravings and aversions. *Journal of Nutrition* 133: 835–837.

13. Ashtami is the eighth day of the Hindu lunar calendar, observed with religious practice.

14. Schultz, W. (2000). Multiple reward signals in the brain. *Nature Reviews: Neuroscience* 1: 199–207.

8. THE SIXTH LAW OF HAPPINESS

1. Kahneman, D., and J. Snell. (1992). Predicting a changing taste: Do people know what they will like? *Journal of Behavioral Decision Making* 5(3): 187–200.

2. We take the term *presentism* from Gilbert, who has eloquently argued that predictions of future emotions and states of mind are heavily influenced by our current emotions and states of mind. Economists have also discovered this tendency, and call it *projection bias.* See Loewenstein, G., T. O'Donoghue, and M. Rabin. (2003). Projection bias in predicting future utility. *Quarterly Journal of Economics* 118: 1209–1248.

3. Gottman, J. M., and N. Silver. (1999). *The Seven Principles for Making Marriage Work.* New York: Three Rivers Press.

4. Nisbett, R. E., and D. E. Kanouse. (1968). Obesity, hunger, and supermarket shopping behavior. *Proceedings of the Annual Convention of the American Psychological Association* 3: 683–684. See also Gilbert, D. T., M. J. Gill, and T. D. Wilson. (1992). The future is now: Temporal correction in affective forecasting. *Organizational Behavior and Human Decision Processes* 88(1): 430–444.

5. Mischel, W. (1974). Process in delay of gratification. Advances in Experimental Social Psychology 7: 249–292.

6. Malcolm Gladwell is the author of bestsellers such as *The Tipping Point: How Little Things Can Make a Big Difference* (2000) and *Blink: The Power of Thinking without Thinking* (2005). He is a journalist who has been working for the *New Yorker* since 1996.

7. Antonio Damasio, internationally recognized as a leader in the field of neuroscience, is the David Dornsife Professor of Neuroscience and the director of the Brain and Creativity Institute at the University of Southern California. His research area is the neurobiology of mind and behavior, with an emphasis on emotion, decision making, memory, communication, and creativity.

8. To rely on others' direct experience is one of the main messages of the bestseller *Stumbling on Happiness,* by Daniel Gilbert. Daniel Gilbert is a professor of psychology at Harvard University. Gilbert claims that our beliefs about what makes us happy are often wrong because our brain misjudges what will make us satisfied, and that humans are wildly resilient, even regarding happiness. For an interesting presentation, see his TED talk "Why Are We Happy?"

9. Baba Shiv is a professor of marketing at the Graduate School of Business at Stanford University. His research focuses on how the average consumer is influenced by environmental factors, and how many of these factors are nonconscious. In his opinion, emotions are key in the decision-making process and offer insights for advertising, brand strategies, and marketing.

9. THE TREASURE OF HAPPINESS

1. Roper-Starch Organization. (1979). Roper Reports 79–1. Roper Center, University of Connecticut, Storrs.

2. Roper-Starch Organization. (1995). Roper Reports 95–1. Roper Center, University of Connecticut, Storrs.

3. Schmuck, P., and K. Sheldon. (2001). *Life Goals and Well-Being: Toward a Positive Psychology of Human Striving.* Seattle: Hogrefe & Huber.

4. Dittmar, H. (1992). *The Social Psychology of Material Possessions: To Have Is to Be.* Upper Saddle River, NJ: Prentice Hall.

5. Lotto winner's burger bar return. *BBC News,* March 28, 2008.

6. Scitovsky, T. (1976). *The Joyless Economy.* Oxford: Oxford University Press. 1976.

7. Schulz, R., and S. Decker. (1985). Long-term adjustment to physical disability: The role of social support, perceived control and self-blame. *Journal of Personality and Social Psychology* 48: 1162–1172. See also Brickman, P., D. Coates, and R. Janoff-Bulman. (1978). Lottery winners and accident victims: Is happiness relative? *Journal of Personality and Social Psychology* 36: 917–927.

8. Veenhoven, R. (1999). Quality of life in individualistic society: A comparison of 43 nations in the early 1990's. *Social Indicators Research* 48: 157–186.

9. Chan, R., and S. Joseph. (2000). Dimensions of personality, domains of aspiration and subjective well-being. *Personality and Individual Differences* 28: 347–354; Inglehart, R., and J. Rabier. (1986). Aspirations adapt to situations—but why are the Belgians so much happier than the French? In *Research on the Quality of Life,* ed. F. M. Andrews, pp. 1–56. Ann Arbor: Institute for Social Research, University of Michigan.

10. Epicurus (341–270 BCE) was an ancient Greek philosopher and the founder of Epicureanism, a philosophy concerned with the attainment of happiness. He taught that pleasure and pain are the measures of what is good and evil, that death is the end of the body and the soul and should therefore not be feared, that the gods do not reward or punish humans, that the universe is infinite and eternal, and that events in the world are ultimately based on the motions and interactions of atoms moving in empty space.

11. Kabat-Zinn, J. (1990). *Full Catastrophe Living: Using the Wisdom of Your Mind to Face Stress, Pain, and Illness.* New York: Delacorte Press.

12. Paloma, M., and B. Pendleton. (1990). Religious domains and general well-being. *Social Indicators Research* 19: 60–67.

13. Transcribed from Norman Cousins's "Talk on Positive Emotions and Health," first aired in 1983 on public radio station KCRW-FM in Santa Monica, California.

10. CUMULATIVE COMPARISON

1. Carol Ryff, at the University of Wisconsin, is involved in a large-scale well-being research project on happiness titled Midlife in the United States, or MIDUS II, which attempts to answer whether well-being and ill-being, such as depression, have distinct biological correlates or are at opposite ends of the same psychological spectrum. See Ryff, C. D. (1989). Happiness is everything, or is it? Explorations on the meaning of psychological well-being. *Journal of Personality and Social Psychology* 57(6): 1069–1081.

2. The mathematics of cumulative goods works as follows. Suppose that the levels of reality have been $R(1)$, $R(2)$, ..., $R(t)$, where t stands for the current period. Then, consider the levels of accumulated reality so far, that is:

$$A(t) = R(1) + R(2) + \ldots + R(t).$$

In period t, the happiness seismogram takes the following value:

$$\text{Happiness}(t) = H(\, A(t) - E(t)\,),$$

Where $H()$ is the happiness S-curve. In this case, expectations chase the *accumulated* level of reality, that is:

$$E(t+1) = E(t) + \text{Speed of Adaptation} \times (\, A(t) - E(t)\,).$$

This implies that if we stop accumulating, then the accumulated level will stay constant, expectations will eventually match this level, and happiness will revert to zero.

3. Ignacio Carreras is a patron of Fundacion Lealtad, an organization that audits multiple nongovernmental organizations. He argues that most people like to make donations to buildings or tangible goods because they like to see the results. Donors who strongly identify with the cause may give to operating expenses such as salaries for teachers or doctors.

4. Warr, P. (1978). A study of psychological well-being. *British Journal of Psychology* 69: 111–121.

5. Payne, R. (1988). A longitudinal study of the psychological well-being of unemployed men and the mediating effect of neuroticism. *Human Relations* 41: 119–138.

6. Freedman, J., and P. Shaver. (1975). What makes you happy—Questionnaire. *Psychology Today* 9(5): 66–72; Freedman, J. (1978). *Happy People*. New York: Harcourt Brace Jovanovich.

7. Argyle, M., and B. Beit-Hallahmi. (1997). *The Psychology of Religious Behaviour, Belief and Experience*. London: Routledge.

8. Little, B., and I. McGregor. (1998). Personal projects, happiness, and meaning: On doing well and being yourself. *Journal of Personality and Social Psychology* 74: 494–512.

9. John Michael Argyle (1925–2002), a social psychologist, is the author of more than twenty-five books on a wide variety of topics. He was a pioneer in the study of social psychology in Britain, always making sure that the findings could be translated for practical use. See Argyle, J. (2001). *The Psychology of Happiness*. New York: Routledge.

10. In 1951, Erna Barschak published a study of happiness and unhappiness in childhood and adolescence of girls in different cultures after interviewing more than four hundred girls in England, Switzerland, and the United States, among other countries. See Barschak, E. (1951). A study of happiness and unhappiness in childhood and adolescence of girls in different cultures. *Journal of Psychology* 32: 173–215.

11. Glenn, N. (1975). The contributions of marriage to the psychological well-being of males and females. *Journal of Marriage and Family Relations* 37: 594–600.

12. The prisoner's dilemma is a game that leads to mistrust and a worse payoff for both players. The original story goes like this. Bonnie and Clyde are arrested on the suspicion of robbing a bank. They are placed in separate cells and each is given the following deal. "If you confess to the crime, and the other person does not confess, then you will be set free and the other person will be sent to prison for ten years. If both of you confess to the crime, each of you will get a moderate sentence of two years in prison. If neither of you confesses, then you each will get six months in prison." If Bonnie and Clyde trust each other, then they will not confess and each will get away with a six-month sentence. If either of them mistrusts the other, however, then each will confess, hoping to avoid ten years in prison, but each of them risks suffering a two-year prison sentence instead.

13. Gottman, J.M., and N. Silver. (1999). *The Seven Principles for Making Marriage Work*. New York: Three Rivers Press.

14. Milton, J. ([1667] 2008). *Paradise Lost*. Edited by R. C. Flannagan. Oxford: Oxford University Press.

II. REFRAMING

1. Viktor Frankl (1905–1997) wrote a total of thirty-two books on existential analysis and logotherapy, which have been translated into twenty-six languages. He taught at several universities, including Vienna, Harvard, and Stanford. The book *Man's Search for Meaning*, which sold approximately nine million copies worldwide, is one of the ten most influential books of the twentieth century, according to the Library of Congress. Frankl said: "There is nothing in the world, I venture to say, that would so effectively help one to survive even the worst conditions as the knowledge that there is a meaning in one's life." See Frankl, V. (1998). *Man's Search for Meaning*. New York: Washington Square Press.

2. Genes account for 50 percent of the variability in happiness across individuals. The 50 percent attributed to genetic factors is puzzling. The evidence is strong, but there are multiple interpretations of the evidence. In light of our framework, we can think of three competing explanations:

1. Differences in happiness set point. The neutral state to which we tend to revert after adaptation is genetically determined and this set point varies across individuals. That is, genes determine the position on the map of emotions on which the butterfly settles while resting.

2. The law of motion of expectations is genetically determined and differs across individuals. For instance, genes may determine the speed of adaptation, the tendency to engage in social comparison, or the ability to reframe adverse situations.

3. It has been well documented that character traits, such as extroversion, are genetically determined and differ across individuals. Because it costs less for extroverts to make new friends, they end up with more friends. As social interaction is a basic good, extroverts end up being happier (not because they are extroverts but because they have more friends). Other traits of character such as general intelligence may influence happiness indirectly, as it may correlate with our degree of presentism and impatience.

If the first explanation is correct, then we are left to conclude that 50 percent of our happiness is already decided by our genes and another 15 percent by our circumstances. Still, the other 35 percent depends on our choices.

If the second or third explanation is correct, then in principle we can all be equally happy, although the cost and resources required to be happy differ across individuals. If an introvert were to have the same number of friends, then the introvert would be as happy as the extrovert. The same idea applies to developing mechanisms to avoid social comparison, compensate for the effects of presentism, or reframe reality. The fact that some people are genetically predisposed does not mean that the rest cannot learn.

For references, see Lykken, D. (1999). What Studies on Twins Show Us about Nature and the Happiness Set Point. New York: Golden Books; and Davidson, R. (2003). Affective neuroscience and psychophysiology: Toward a synthesis. *Psychophysiology* 40(5): 655–665.

3. Hastorf, A., and H. Cantril. (1954). They saw a game: A case study. *Journal of Abnormal and Social Psychology* 49: 129–134.

4. Chen, H., and A. Rao. (2002). Close encounters of two kinds: False alarms and dashed hopes. *Marketing Science* 21(2): 160–177.

5. Tversky, A., and D. Griffin. (1991). Endowment and contrast in judgments of well-being. In *Subjective Well-Being: An Interdisciplinary Perspective,* ed. F. Strack, M. Argyle, and N. Schwarz, pp. 108–118. Oxford: Pergamon.

6. Joan Miró in a letter to J. F. Ràfols, in Joan Miró. (1987). *Selected Writings and Interviews.* Edited by Margit Rowell. London: Thames and Hudson.

7. In the actual study, customers were given the opportunity to taste samples and then were offered a one-dollar discount if they decided to make a purchase. When six varieties of the jam were made available, 30 percent of the costumers actually bought a jar, whereas when twenty-four varieties were available, more people came to the table but only 3 percent of them bought a jar.

8. A good reference is the book *Simple Heuristics That Make Us Smart,* edited by Gerd Gigerenzer, Peter M. Todd, and the ABC Research Group. That elimination by aspects chooses the best alternative with high probability is demonstrated in Baucells, M., J. A. Carrasco, and R. M. Hogarth. (2008). Cumulative dominance and heuristic performance in binary multi-attribute choice. *Operations Research* 56(5): 1289–1304. However, elimination by aspects is not bulletproof, as it may eliminate a candidate who is very good by all criteria except the first one.

9. See John Wooden's TED talk with the title "On the Difference between Winning and Success."

10. Ariely, D. (2008). *Predictably Irrational: The Hidden Forces That Shape Our Decisions.* New York: HarperCollins. Multiple examples on how adding inferior alternatives may alter choices are given in Dan Ariely's TED talk with the title "Are We in Control of Our Own Decisions?"

11. Tolle, E. (1999). *The Power of Now: A Guide to Spiritual Enlightenment.* Novato, CA: New World Library.

12. Thich Nhat Hanh. (2002). *Anger: Wisdom for Cooling the Flames.* New York: Riverhead Trade.

13. Seligman, M. E. P. (2002). *Authentic Happiness: Using the New Positive Psychology to Realize Your Potential for Lasting Fulfillment.* New York: Free Press.

14. Michael Norton of Harvard University and his colleagues have documented that prosocial behavior increases happiness. The authors suggest that how people spend their money may be at least as important as how much money they earn. Specifically, they hypothesize that spending money on other people may have a more positive impact on happiness than spending money on oneself. See Dunn, E. W., L. B. Aknin, and M. I. Norton. (2008). Spending money on others promotes happiness. *Science* 319: 1687–1688.

15. Richard Thaler is a professor of behavioral sciences and economics at the University of Chicago Booth School of Business. He proposed that people use mental accounts for making decisions. These accounts serve to associate income sources with expense categories.

12. LIVING WITHIN THE LAWS OF HAPPINESS

1. Matthieu Ricard has a PhD in cellular genetics. He converted to Buddhism and now lives in Shechen Monastery in Nepal, also acting as French interpreter for the Dalai Lama. He is the author of *Happiness: A Guide to Developing Life's Most Important Skill.* New York: Little, Brown, 2006. This citation is taken from his TED talk with the title "On the Habits of Happiness."

2. Easterlin, R. (2003). Explaining happiness. *Proceedings of the National Academy of Sciences* 100(19): 11176–11183.

3. We are assuming that Adam spends all that he earns within the same year. But this assumption, called narrow bracketing, does not change the direction of the results presented.

INDEX

Italicized page numbers indicate figures and tables.

activities, 68. *See also* adaptive goods; basic goods; goods
adaptation: basic goods and, 131–32; to change and, 61–64; to life circumstances and, 64–66; lottery winners and, 83, 86; partial and, 66–67; presentism, and bias of, 113–15; social relationships and, 115; speed of, 81, 185, 215n4. *See also* adaptation conquest; adaptive goods; diminishing sensitivity
adaptation bias, 113–15. *See also* presentism
adaptation conquest: adaptive goods transformation and, 160–61; bad things sometimes happen and, 163–64; broader comparison and, 161; choice anxiety and, 164–66, 222nn7–8; detachment and, 161–63; emotional regulation and, 167; expectation management and, 159; motion of expectation and, 61–64; optimism and, 166–67; reality contrasts as favorable and, 159–60. *See also* adaptation
adaptive goods: cumulative goods transformation from and, 160–61; life balance chakra and, 191–92; living within Laws of Happiness and, 182–83; motion of expectation and,

69. *See also* adaptation; adaptation conquest
age, and happiness, 13
anticipation, 37–39, 41, 185–86. *See also* defining happiness; living within Laws of Happiness
Argyle, Michael, 144, 145, 147–48, 220n9
Ariely, Dan, 165–66
Aristotle, ix, 105–6
Ashtami, 108, 216n13. *See also* India
aversion to loss. *See* loss aversion
Ayres, Ian, 74

bad things sometimes happen, 163–64, 196, 202
balance, *187*, 187–93, 191–92, 197, 204, 223n3. *See also* building a happier life; living within Laws of Happiness
Barschak, Erna, 148, 220n10
basic goods: overview, 127–29, 137; adaptation and, 131–32; bodily needs and, 132–34; concrete guidelines and, 137; conspicuous goods and, 128, 130; description of, 129–31; goods defined and, 68; heart needs and, 134–36; life balance chakra and, 191; living within Laws of Happiness and, 181; lottery winners and, 129; mind's needs and, 132, 136–37; motion

contrasts, 159–60. *See also* reality
coping strategies for loss, 90–91,
   215nn5–6. *See also* diminishing
   sensitivity; loss aversion
Cousins, Norman, 137
cravings, 106–9. *See also* satiation
crescendo (less-to-more): building a
   happier life and, 196, 201; diminishing
   sensitivity and, 88, 89, 91–92, 95;
   motion of expectation and, 64;
   variety with and, 103–4, 186. *See also*
   diminishing sensitivity; incremental
   technological improvement
   ("reverse brave new world")
Csíkszentmihályi, Mihály, 21, 209n16
culture, and happiness, 13, 18, 208n1,
   208n4
cumulation, 197, 203. *See also* building
   a happier life; cumulative goods
   (cumulative comparison)
cumulative goods (cumulative
   comparison): overview, 138–43,
   140, 219n2; adaptive goods
   transformation into, 160–61;
   concrete guidelines and, 154;
   confession and, 152–53; definition
   of, 69–70; forgiveness and, 151–53;
   goals and, 143, 145–48; life balance
   chakra and, 191; living within Laws
   of Happiness and, 182; memories
   and, 153; pleasure and, 203; positive
   and negative sides of, 143–45; reality
   and expectations comparison and,
   138–42, *140*; resentment and, 151–53;
   seismogram for happiness and, 144;
   social relationships and, 143, 148–53;
   trust as, 149–51, 220n12. *See also* basic
   goods; cumulation; reframing

Daly, Mary, 22
Damasio, Antonio, 120, 217n7
Darwin, Charles, 28, 59, 133–34
Davidson, Richard, 25–26, 210n23
day reconstruction method, 18–20. *See
   also* measuring happiness

defining happiness: overview, 27–28,
   29, 30, 42–43; anticipation and,
   37–39, 41; happydons and, 32, 34;
   map of emotions and, 28, *29*, 30,
   211nn2–3; moment-happiness and,
   30; operational and, 30–32, 211nn4–5,
   212n6; recall of past events and,
   39–42. *See also* seismogram for
   happiness
Denmark, 18, 135
detachment, 161–63. *See also* adaptation
   conquest
diaries studies, 23. *See also* measuring
   happiness
Dickens, Charles, 47, 60
Diener, Ed, 12, 208n1
diminishing sensitivity: overview,
   78–79, 95; concrete guidelines and,
   92–95; consumption decisions test
   and, 82–89, 214n3, 215nn5–6; coping
   strategies for loss and, 90–91,
   215nn5–6; crescendo and, 88, 89,
   91–92, 95; incremental technological
   improvement and, 92–95; lottery
   winners and, 78; optimizing
   happiness and, 80–82, 214n2;
   S-curve of happiness and, 79–80,
   80, 215n4
Duchenne smile, 24, 210n21

Easterlin, Richard, 5
Edgeworth, Francis, 32
Ekman, Paul, 24, 210n20
Elster, Jon, 37–38
emotions: diversification of, 187–88;
   emotions of the moment and, 119–21;
   life narratives for emotional cancellation and, 176–79, 223n15; map
   of, 28, *29*, 30, 211nn2–3; pain and, 3, *5*,
   6, 27, 136, 218n10; reframing, 176–79,
   223n15; regulation of, 167. *See also*
   pleasure
employment (work), 115, 144, 157, 176,
   184, 189, 196, 199. *See also* building a
   happier life

happier life; motion of expectation; reframing
Hogarth, R. M., 222n8
Hume, David, 120
Huxley, Aldous, 92

income, 13, 15–18, *16,* 193. *See also* lottery winners; measuring happiness
incremental technological improvement ("reverse brave new world"), 92–95
India: Ashtami and, 108, 216n13; cravings and, 108; defining happiness and, 40; *Kama Sutra* and, 168, 174; *Mahabharata* and, 54–55; reframing and, 161, 172, 173, 178; social comparison and, 50, 168

James, William, 5
Jevons, William Stanley, 39
Johnson, Samuel, 101

Kabat-Zinn, Jon, 136
Kahneman, Daniel: defining happiness and, 40, 212n6; Loss Aversion and, 72, 214n1; measurement for happiness and, 18, 209n14; motion of expectation and, 213n1; presentism and, 111–12; science of happiness and, 3
Kama Sutra, 168, 174
Karlan, Dean, 74
karma yoga, 162
Kelvin, William Thomas, 11
Killingsworth, Matthew A., 21
Kushner, Harold, 163

Lamarck, Jean-Baptiste, 194
laughter therapy, 137. *See also* smiles and smiling
Law of Hedonic Asymmetry, 72. *See also* loss aversion
Laws of Happiness, 3, 7. *See also* diminishing sensitivity; living within Laws of Happiness; loss

aversion; motion of expectation; presentism; satiation; social comparison (relative comparison)
Lazarus Richard, 211n3
less-to-more (crescendo). *See* crescendo (less-to-more); diminishing sensitivity; incremental technological improvement ("reverse brave new world")
levels of stress (body measurements), 12, 24–25, 210n21. *See also* measuring happiness
life balance chakra, *187,* 187–93, 223n3. *See also* balance; living within Laws of Happiness
life circumstances, adaptation to, 64–66. *See also* motion of expectation
life narratives for emotional cancellation, 176–79, 223n15. *See also* reframing
life simplicity of few habituating goods, 104–6. *See also* habituating goods; satiation
Little, Brian, 146
living within Laws of Happiness: overview, 180–81, *187;* adaptation speed and, 185; adaptive goods and, 182–83; anticipation and, 185–86; basic goods and, 181; concrete guidelines and, 193; conspicuous goods and, 185; cumulative goods and, 182; emotional diversification and, 187–88; income and, 193; life balance chakra and, *187,* 187–93, 223n3; lottery winners and, 188; recall and, 185–86; reframing and, 181–82, 184–85; social comparison goods and, 183–84; social relationships and, 184; spiritual practices and, 186; variety with crescendo and, 186. *See also* building a happier life
Locke, John, 71
Loewenstein, George, 37–38

Text:	10.75/15 Janson
Display:	Janson MT Pro
Compositor:	Toppan Best-set Premedia Limited
Indexer:	J. Naomi Linzer
Printer and Binder:	Maple-Vail Book Manufacturing Group